Surviving the Girl Next Door

K. P. Goodwin

Published by K. P. Goodwin, 2024.

SURVIVING THE GIRL NEXT DOOR

First edition. December 18, 2024.

ISBN: 979-8230512462

Written by K. P. Goodwin.

Table of Contents

Dedication

If you have ever been betrayed by someone you trusted more than anyone else in life, this book is dedicated to you.

"All I know is that sometimes

you have to be wary

Of a miracle too good to be true

All I know is that sometimes

the truth is contrary

Everything in life you thought you knew

All I know is that sometimes

you have to be wary

'Cause sometimes

the target is you"

Neil Peart

Two Tragedies, Part I

Oscar Wilde has been quoted as saying, "There are only two tragedies in life: one is not getting what one wants, and the other is getting it." As a young man, I had no idea that these words would one day have such a profound impact on my life.

Like many young boys, I started playing guitar at age twelve. By age thirteen, after learning a few songs, I began playing in my first garage band with two other neighborhood kids, Steve and Joey. Steve also played guitar, and Joey played drums. We didn't have a bass player, but it didn't seem to matter, and it probably wasn't going to make a big difference at that point in our musical endeavors.

Sadly, after playing a couple of small parties, I learned that my family would be moving away, and this would be the end of our band. It would not, however, be the end of my musical dreams.

After moving from Oklahoma to Missouri, I made friends with some kids who were more into riding dirt bikes than playing guitar. Fortunately for me, and because doctors didn't tend to put so many hyper kids on medication back in the day, my parents found other ways to keep me occupied. This included a go-cart at age seven, a minibike at eight, and my first motorcycle at eleven. Now, alongside my new friends, I spent most of my free time riding and racing dirt bikes, which meant that the guitar would have to wait.

And then it happened. A new band from Queens, New York began taking over the world. And they definitely had my attention. The band was KISS, and they were the most unbelievable thing I had ever seen. In fact, after learning about them I immediately purchased a cheap bass guitar and began learning to play. Although I credit Gene Simmons for turning me on to the bass, I also credit Geddy Lee of the band RUSH for inspiring me to become a better bassist.

Despite stating that I had no plans of ever marrying or having children, several years later, at the age of twenty-two, I had been married for over a year and was back living in Oklahoma. During the day I worked in the oil field for a company called TOTCO, and on the weekends I played with a hard-rock band called Crystal. Unfortunately, within a couple of years, both had gone bust.

Because we needed the money to survive, I begrudgingly joined a country band called Fantasy, which kept me busy on the weekends and helped pay the bills. At the time, all my experience had been with rock bands, so it was a difficult transition and eventually led to me being fired for being "too progressive" for their taste. At the time, it was a hard blow to my pride and my finances, but as luck would have it, things were about to take a turn for the better.

Shortly after being released from the band, I met a drummer named Randy, who was not only a great drummer but was also a good friend to have around. He, too, was looking for work, so he brought his drums over and we began jamming together. It didn't take long before we decided it was time to audition guitarists and lead vocalists. Then, after a couple of failed auditions, I got a call from a friend who was working in a local music store. He told me that a guitarist/vocalist named Larry had a four-night gig coming up, and he needed a drummer and a bassist to back him up. This sounded almost too good to be true, but Randy and I were definitely interested.

Larry showed up at the house on Monday just before noon, and we began rehearsing for the gig, which was to begin on Wednesday night. We knew it would be cutting it close, but we all needed the work, and at that point in our musical careers, we three knew how to play a lot of the same material.

After rehearsing for several hours on Monday, all day on Tuesday, and a few hours on Wednesday, we loaded up our equipment and headed to the club. A little uneasy about how it would all turn out, we never would have guessed that it was going to go so well for us.

It was obvious that we were all a little nervous right out of the gate, but it didn't take us long to settle down and enjoy the experience. Then, to our surprise, on our third night of playing at the club, the manager offered us a job as the house band. We couldn't believe our luck. This was a dream job for three young musicians looking to break into the music business. And, for the first time in my life, at the age of twenty-four, I was a working, professional musician.

Sadly, I've since learned that nothing good lasts forever, at least not for me.

Within less than two years, my wife at the time, Vonda, wanted me to make a career change and become a white-collar professional. She got the idea from a co-worker whose husband had just graduated with a computer-related degree from a community college and immediately began working in the computer industry. It was not something that I was interested in doing, but I have since learned that people-pleasing is one of my character flaws, and rarely does it work out in my best interest. So, at the age of twenty-six, I walked away from the band. My wife and I moved from Lawton back up to Oklahoma City, and I started taking computer-related classes at the community college. I also had my first back surgery that year. It was not a good year for me.

I attended school full time, worked a part-time job and put my musical aspirations on hold for two years until I graduated with an associate degree. After graduating, I was fortunate enough to get a job with the University of Oklahoma, College of Continuing Education, where I would work for the next sixteen years. Because the position was through a government contract with the Federal Aviation Administration, I worked at the Mike Monroney Aeronautical Center.

I had done exactly what was asked of me and was working in a white-collar position as a computer programmer. Then it was time to find a band and get back to playing music. But I didn't know that Vonda had other ideas. Shortly after I began working for the University of Oklahoma, Vonda informed me that she wanted to start a family. I reminded her that although I relented and got married, I still had no plans of having children. I now understand that would have been the perfect time to stop being a people-pleaser and to learn how to say no to others. But, because I didn't, I once again relented and gave in to her wishes. Although I now would make a different decision, I want to say that I can't imagine a world without my children in it. I have also since learned that not saying no to people would alter the course of my life in ways that I couldn't imagine at the time.

We purchased a home in Yukon, Oklahoma, started a family, and I returned to playing music. I bounced around with a couple of bands before meeting Robby and Rory, who were looking for a bassist and lead vocalist. I later met Mark at an open-mic jam session, and he became the last piece of the puzzle. Our band, Hired Guns, a progressive-country band, played together throughout the late 1980s and early 1990s. We became the house band at Ernie's Palace and occasionally played as headliners at the Diamond Ballroom, which was a big deal back in those days.

We all wanted to reach the top in the music industry and believed it was a real possibility. We had the talent, we were writing and performing our own music, and we occasionally received requests to play some of our original material. Things were finally coming together for me and our band. The next step was to cut a demo and hope that the right person heard and liked it. We were so close that we could almost taste it. And then all hell broke loose.

Without warning, Vonda blindsided me with a divorce.

"I don't want to be married to someone who is trying to make it in the music business," she calmly stated. "I want you to pursue a career as a computer programmer and move up into a management position."

I tried to explain that I had no desire to pursue a path in management.

"I've done everything that you've asked of me, and I think it's my turn to finish what I've started with the band," I said.

"Then that's your decision to make, but I am divorcing you."

The band was booked to play every weekend, including another two dates at the Diamond Ballroom, and I didn't know how to deal with the madness that was crushing my soul. I was finally in a band that had the potential to become successful, but if I stayed in the band, I would never get to spend time with my kids. As a father, I knew what decision had to be made, and I made it.

Although it wouldn't be the last time that my inability to say no to people would cause me a great deal of suffering, it was the first time I truly felt like the world was unfair.

And like so many other people on this planet, I had just experienced the first tragedy of Oscar Wilde's quote about not getting what we want. If only I had known that the second tragedy of his quote was patiently waiting for me in the distant future.

First Encounter

As the dust began to settle from the divorce, and some type of sanity slowly returned to my mind, I started thinking about my future and how I might recover from the loss of everything. Thanks to the divorce, I lost my home and was living in a one-bedroom apartment. I now had only limited access to my children, every other weekend. My financial status was very bleak and would remain this way for what appeared at the time to be the rest of my life. I was so overwhelmed that I had no idea how I was going to overcome so many obstacles.

I finally accepted the fact that if I ever wanted to own a home again or even have enough money to take the kids out for an inexpensive meal, I would need a second income. With this in mind, I began thinking about getting a second job or even returning to school to further my education. I started by brainstorming and writing down anything that popped into my head, regardless of whether it was feasible or not. After creating a long list of possibilities, I took some time to try to wrap my mind around the situation.

At some point, I decided to further my education, which allowed me to remove everything relating to a second job from the list. I then went through the remaining items and eliminated everything that would require me to attend college during the day. Obviously, I couldn't quit my job, which was my only source of income. Therefore, it didn't take too long to narrow the list down to one option that I could do after my regular work hours. Unfortunately, I wasn't sure if it was good for me. The only option remaining on my list was the nursing program offered through the Oklahoma City Community College. At that point in my life, I knew absolutely nothing about nursing or if it was a profession that I could even pursue. I had never before thought about nursing as a career. However, what has been said about desperate times calling for desperate measures was certainly true in my life at that time.

After researching further, I met with an advisor to discuss the requirements and possibility of getting into the program. I quickly learned that getting accepted would be no easy task. It turned out that acceptance was based on a points system. Although many of my general education courses would transfer over to the program, it would take me approximately two years of prerequisites just to earn enough points to qualify for the two-year nursing program. And then there was no guarantee that my application would be accepted. I felt hopeless, like I was running into a brick wall at every turn.

A few more weeks had gone by before I sat down and put together a five-year plan. Step one was taking all the prerequisites required for the program. Step two was getting into the nursing program and successfully completing it. And step three would include passing the National Council Licensure Examination (NCLEX), getting my license, and going to work on opposite weekends of having the kids. No problem. I mean, what could go wrong with this plan? Right?

I'm very grateful to be one of those people who require fewer hours of sleep than most. If not for the ability to function on less sleep than the average person, I never would have made it past the first two years of my five-year plan. Fortunately, I completed the prerequisites, got accepted into the nursing program, and completed Nursing Process I and II, which left only Nursing Process III and IV. Each class was one semester, which meant that I had only one year left before completing the entire nursing program and being eligible to sit for the NCLEX.

I'm not sure why, but I feel like I'm continuously being tested by a supreme being in the universe. I don't want to call anyone out because

I don't know who's in charge of it. However, it seems to me that when things are beginning to break my way, something happens and I have to dig a little deeper to keep from failing. Maybe this is how it is for everyone and I'm just not aware of what others are dealing with in their lives. I don't know. But I do know that it seems to happen a lot to me.

With only two classes remaining to complete the nursing program, I learned that I had a ruptured disc and required surgery to correct the problem. Because it was the only option, I had the surgery between semesters and began the recovery process. When it was time to return to class, my body had not fully recovered, and I was still dealing with a lot of pain. I was unsure if I should take off a semester, and it was my dad who suggested that I try going back to class before making a decision. My doctor didn't like the idea of releasing me to work and school so quickly but agreed to do so as long as I didn't lift over ten pounds for several weeks. Luckily, Nursing Process III started with a psychology class and required no lifting of patients. And by the time I started Nursing Process IV, I was feeling pretty well and no longer needed any pain medication.

It was shortly after starting Nursing Process III that I met a lady named Lorrie. Unfortunately, my schedule didn't leave much time for dating. She understood that I still had almost a year of classwork before graduating, and since I hadn't dated in almost four years, she understood that this was not a high priority for me. We did, however, squeeze in some time together during my final year of college.

During the following year, I graduated with my associate degree in nursing, passed the NCLEX and received my license as a registered nurse. For those of you who understand how the NCLEX works and are curious, I completed the test with only seventy-five questions. Now, I needed to find a part-time job, which turned out to be a lot easier than getting into the nursing program. I actually took on two part-time jobs, which, along with my full-time position as a computer programmer, I worked for about a year. And although juggling everything was a little tough at times, it was still easier than working full time and going to nursing school, and the extra income allowed me to pay off the debt that I had incurred. (I didn't qualify for a student loan, so the credit card was my only option.) After paying off my debt, I purchased a small home in Yukon just over a mile from where my kids were living, and then I bought a nearly new SUV. Life was beginning to feel good again.

Yeah, I know what that means, and you're right. But this time, it's not what you're thinking.

I had finally reached the point that I was no longer working a second job, which left me with a lot of free time. I would occasionally pick up a case with an IV therapy company, but not because I desperately needed the money. It was to keep my license active and not lose the skills that I worked so hard to develop.

Most of us are probably familiar with the saying, "Long days and short years." Well, I can honestly say that it's so true for me. Before I realized it, Lorrie and I had been dating for nearly four years, which was just fine with me. And I thought it was good for her, too. After all, I had made it very clear that I would never be married again and had explained the reasons for my decision. Not only was going through a divorce emotionally painful and financially devastating, it was also the reason that I had spent five years of my life working a full-time job while attending school for four of those years and then working three jobs for a year. It was a very difficult time for me, and I just didn't want to put myself in that situation ever again. But I soon learned that Lorrie wasn't content with just dating.

It wasn't the same as learning your spouse wants a divorce or that you need a second back surgery, but it still caught me off-guard when Lorrie gave me an ultimatum.

"I don't want to just date forever," she told me. "I want to get married."

I said, "Lorrie, you know how I feel about marriage. I went through hell when Vonda divorced me, and I just can't put myself in that situation again."

She didn't get upset, but she made her feelings clear. "If you're not willing to get married then we need to call it quits."

That little voice that tries to warn us when we're about to make a bad decision was telling me it was time to hit the brakes, and I was listening to it this time. Unfortunately, the people-pleaser in me said, "I'm going to need to take some time and think about it." Why did I say that to her? I cared for her a great deal, and the kids loved her, but I just didn't want to be married again. She agreed to give me some time to figure out what I was going to do, and the conversation ended there.

I don't recall how much time I took, probably several weeks, before I brought the subject up again.

"I've put a lot of thought into it, and I'm willing to compromise. I'm willing to sell our homes and purchase one together, but I'm not ready to be married or combine our finances. We can open a checking account in both our names and we'll use it to pay the bills, but everything else stays separated. I know it's not exactly what you want, but it's the best I can do."

"Would you be open to the possibility of getting married in the future?" she asked.

"I don't know," I replied, "and I don't want to mislead you."

I don't recall the rest of the conversation, but we agreed to the compromise and began moving forward with our plans. It didn't take long at all for her to sell her condo in Norman, Oklahoma, and we agreed that she should move into my home until we found one to purchase. Everything was moving so fast that within a few weeks, we found and purchased a home just a few blocks from where we were living. After closing the deal and moving into our new home, my house sold within a month, which allowed us to avoid making two house payments. (Okay, sometimes—not often—it does seem like things go my way.)

The next few years were fairly standard and nothing too big went wrong, but we did have the typical issues that involved kids and careers, and although I worked in a state position for Oklahoma University, the Federal Aviation Administration contract was funded by the federal government, which meant that the funding could end at any time without notice. When I began working at the university in March 1987, over five hundred employees were working on the contract. During my interview, I was told that the federal contract brought in more money than the university's football program. But at one point during my employment with the university, the number of employees had dwindled to fewer than thirty before bouncing back and stabilizing at approximately eighty-five employees.

Because of these past experiences, I began rethinking my career and the future. I'm sure it had a lot to do with my age and the fact that I was still a contractor, but I thought it might be the right time to make a career change and move into nursing on a full-time basis. So, after researching a few possibilities, I began thinking that I might be interested in dialysis nursing. It sounded like a specialty of nursing where I would be able to use both my computer and nursing skills. After a couple of interviews with one of the many facilities owned by Fresenius Medical Care, it looked like I was about to be hired by the company. Just as I was about to be offered a position, the facility manager informed me that he was instead offering the position to an experienced dialysis nurse. It wasn't the news that I was expecting, but I definitely understood. After all, training a nurse to work proficiently in dialysis takes a few months.

Another nursing specialty that I was considering was an operating room circulator, and a position was available at Bone and Joint Hospital. After applying and being accepted for the nursing position, I submitted my resignation as a computer programmer and left the university in March 2003. I'm not sure why, but it only dawned on me years later that I had worked exactly sixteen years with the university, beginning and ending in March.

I quickly learned that my new position as an operating room circulator was not a good fit for me. I had made a mistake. Unsure of what to do next, and having only worked a couple of months in the position, I once again began thinking about dialysis nursing. For reasons unclear to me at the time, it felt like I was being drawn toward this specialty of nursing. Later, I would come to believe that the universe has much more control over our lives, including those seemingly insignificant day-to-day decisions, than most of us can begin to understand. You know, that thing called "free will" that we so desperately want to believe we have.

A few days later, I decided to use my lunch break to walk across the street to Saint Anthony Hospital to inquire about their dialysis program. I knew it was a long shot, but I was hopeful that they would have a nursing position open or possibly have one opening up in the near future. At that time, Bone and Joint and Saint Anthony hospitals were connected by an underground tunnel, which allowed me quick access between the two facilities. I only had thirty minutes for my lunch break, so the tunnel was a nice shortcut.

As soon as it was my turn to take a break, I walked over to Saint Anthony Hospital and began looking for the dialysis unit. I don't recall what floor I was on, but it was eerily quiet, with no one around in the long hallway. Then, as fate would have it, a tall, gorgeous nurse in blue scrubs entered the hallway from one of the rooms. We made eye contact, and I began walking toward her. I, too, was wearing scrubs, so I'm fairly sure this made her feel comfortable with me.

"Hi, I'm looking for the dialysis unit and I'm wondering if you might be able to help me," I said to her.

Pointing at the open doorway to the room she had just exited, she replied, "Yes, it's in that room."

I couldn't believe my luck, I had ended up on the right floor, and the only other person in that hallway besides me was a beautiful, soft-spoken dialysis nurse. I didn't know it at the time, but one day this lovely lady would enter my life and change everything about it beyond belief.

The Year of Change

Upon entering the dialysis unit, I found one patient on dialysis and one nurse sitting at the nurse's station. I introduced myself and explained that I was seeking a dialysis nursing position. The nurse's name was Maria, and after she explained to me that this was the acute dialysis unit, she immediately began recruiting me, which took me by surprise. However, after she realized that I was seeking a position with a more stable work schedule, she provided me with Christie's name and number. Christie was the nurse manager over the chronic dialysis unit, which was also located in Saint Anthony Hospital. I thanked the nurse and quickly returned to work at Bone and Joint Hospital.

I didn't understand how it all worked at the time, but I had learned that the chronic dialysis unit was located on the third floor in the same hospital as the acute dialysis unit and that both units functioned under the care of staff provided by Fresenius Medical Care.

Excited about obtaining the nurse manager's phone number, I reached out to Christie that same day to see if she had any unfilled nursing positions. Fortunately for me, the chronic dialysis unit was in need of another registered nurse. So, after a short conversation with Christie, I scheduled an interview with her.

When I arrived for the interview a couple of days later, I was met by Christie and the area manager, Mark. We spoke for about an hour and, before leaving the interview, I was offered the position. I couldn't believe how well everything had gone the past few days. It really seemed like good fortune was coming my way.

The next day, I submitted my resignation to Bone and Joint Hospital and apologized that I felt the need to make a change so quickly. The charge nurse, whose name I can't remember, was kind and explained that she understood completely. She said that although she loved working in the operating room, she knew that it was not for everyone and wished me the very best. I worked the next two weeks with Bone and Joint Hospital, said my goodbyes and never looked back.

When I accepted the position with Fresenius Medical Care, I explained to Christie that I had a trip to Montana planned with Lorrie's family and asked if it would be possible to start upon returning home. Because the dialysis classes began every two weeks, it worked out perfectly, and I started the new position on Monday following our return home on Saturday. I didn't know it at the time, but only a month later I would realize how fortunate I was to be able to take the trip to Montana with Lorrie's family.

During our trip, Lorrie and I learned that her mother, Sue, who had been diagnosed with dementia, was now much worse than we realized. We didn't know until then that Lorrie's dad, John, had been keeping Sue's failing health secret from the rest of us. If not for spending so much time together every day, we would have continued believing that she was still doing fairly well. It was during the trip to Montana that we witnessed just how confused she became and how quickly John stepped in to help her.

On Monday, after returning home from our trip, I started training for my new position with Fresenius Medical Care. I spent the next two weeks in class before beginning work in the chronic dialysis unit at Saint Anthony Hospital. I know it was a lot of change for Lorrie and me, but I believe it was Lorrie who was dealing with the most change in her life. After working for the University of Oklahoma for sixteen years, I had switched positions twice within a few months, which was definitely very stressful. But Lorrie was not only dealing with the changes that I had made over the past few months, she was now also dealing with her mother's failing health and how it was affecting her father. I think these were the reasons it became so important to her that we get married. Although that little voice kept reminding me that I did not want to be married again, I kept reminding myself that we'd been living together as if we were married for almost five years, and marriage was something that was very important to her. Knowing everything I now know, I would have listened to that little voice and made a different decision. But I didn't. So, with a quick trip to Las Vegas, on June 27, 2003, we got married.

We chose this date because it was exactly five years earlier, on this very day, that we began living together as if we were married. Because only her dad and my parents knew the truth about our living arrangement, we didn't tell anyone about the marriage except the three of them. Only the five of us knew the truth. Soon, it would only be the four of us.

On July 4, 2003, we celebrated John's sixty-ninth birthday. We had no idea it would be the last celebration we would ever have with him. On July 9, five days after his birthday and twelve days after Lorrie and I got married, John died of a heart attack. I had no reason to think about it this way until many years later, but his was the first death to occur after my first encounter with the beautiful nurse I had recently met in the hallway of Saint Anthony Hospital.

After John's death, our lives changed drastically. Lorrie's mother could no longer be left alone, which meant we had to find someone to be with her at all times. Thinking she would do better in a familiar environment, we decided to keep her in her home.

For the first several months, we hired a family member to stay with Sue during the week. Lorrie and I would then spend alternate weekends with Sue, and Lorrie's sister Evon and her husband, Lloyd, would stay on opposite weekends. It was not easy, but we made it work. However, when the situation began taking a toll on Evon's health, we decided to place Sue in a facility where she could receive around-the-clock care. This decision was not an easy one to make, but we believed it was the best for everyone involved.

Because 2003 was such a tough year for so many of us, we were hopeful that 2004 would be a better year. Here's to hoping.

The Favor

This is probably a good time to mention the Allen Saunders' quote (although it is often attributed to John Lennon) that was first published in a 1957 issue of Reader's Digest: "Life is what happens to you while you're busy making other plans."

This brings me back to free will. I often question if it really exists. If I were clairvoyant or had a crystal ball, would I have made different decisions? And, if I had made different decisions, would the outcome be different? Or would the universe still have found a way to force me to fulfill my destiny, regardless of what decisions I made? These are questions that I've pondered for many years, and I've reached the conclusion that I'll probably never have the answers. At least not in this lifetime.

At any rate, 2004 was off to a good start both professionally and personally. I was feeling comfortable with my job as a dialysis nurse, Lorrie and I had recently purchased five acres west of Yukon and we had hired someone to begin building us a new home. It seemed like life was settling down, and we were grateful for the lower stress levels.

After I had worked in dialysis for about six months, Mark, the area manager, approached me with an offer too good to resist. If I was willing to work at any of the locations he managed whenever there was a need for a nurse, he would increase my pay significantly. Without hesitation, I agreed to take on the task. I thought that it would prove to be a good career move, and it did. After only a few months in the new float position, I learned that a charge nurse position would soon be opening up in one of the facilities in Mark's area. Before word got out to everyone in the company, I asked him if he would consider me for the position. Just as I had done for him, without hesitation he assured me that if I wanted the position, it was mine. Therefore, the position was never posted and I moved into the facility as one of the two charge nurses. I had worked at the facility several times, so I was very familiar with all the employees and got along great with them. As it turned out, it was an easy transition, and I really enjoyed working at the smaller facility.

I had been working in the charge nurse position for several months when a new position opened up in the Education Department. I didn't think I had been with Fresenius long enough to qualify for the position until I read the minimum requirements. As it turned out, only one year of dialysis experience was required, and I had about fourteen months with the company at that time. I knew I would be up against other nurses with a lot more experience. However, I had something that many of the other nurses could not list on their resumé. I had sixteen years with the University of Oklahoma, College of Continuing Education developing computer-based training for air traffic controllers, and I had actual classroom experience. I knew it would be a long shot, but I decided to apply for the position. After all, the worst-case scenario would be that I didn't get called in for an interview and would continue working in my current position.

Because Mark had been so good to me, before I submitted my application, I reached out to let him know of my intentions. I wasn't sure how he would feel about my plans, but I knew it was the right thing to do. I was a little nervous when I called him, but he immediately put me at ease when he thanked me for reaching out to him. He encouraged me to apply for the position and wished me the very best. Mark is one of the nicest people I've encountered in my lifetime, so I guess I should have expected nothing less from him.

After updating my resumé, I submitted my application for the position and waited as patiently as possible. I kept telling myself not to be too disappointed if I didn't hear back, but most of us understand that's much easier said than done. To make matters worse, apart from the typical scuttlebutt that seemed to always make the rounds, there was no information getting out from the Education Department. So, like everyone else who had applied for the position, I did my best to forget about it and keep busy.

Another couple of months had gone by when, to my surprise, I received a call from Marsha, the director of education, inquiring if I was still interested in the position. I assured her that I was still very interested and, just like that, I had an interview scheduled with her. I had no idea how many other nurses would be interviewing for the position, but I knew that I had an interview, and that's where I had to focus my attention.

After I had interviewed with Marsha, everything went quiet again. Although the rumor mill was once again churning out a lot of noise, nothing official was getting out of the Education Department. It was several more weeks before I received a call from Marsha. When she told me her decision, I wasn't sure if I had heard her correctly. It took me a minute before I realized she had just offered me the teaching position in the Education Department.

I'm grateful that I maintained my composure and accepted her offer before she changed her mind and offered it to another nurse. She advised me not to discuss her decision with anyone until the following week, allowing her enough time to contact the other applicants. I was working when she called, so it was fortunate that everyone was busy and no one overheard. As much as I wanted to scream it out to everyone, I kept quiet about it for the remainder of the day. Well, at least until I got home that evening.

The start date of my new position was growing closer, but I was still working at the chronic dialysis facility when I received a call from Christy asking me for a favor. Because Christy was the one who originally interviewed me and offered me a position in her dialysis clinic, I would have done just about anything for her. We had become friends since our first meeting, and I consider her a friend to this day.

After catching her up on everything, including my new position in the Education Department, she said, "I need to ask you for a favor."

"Sure, what do you need?" I asked.

"I need to know if you will show one of our nurses how a chronic unit operates?" she said. "She has years of dialysis experience in acutes, but she's looking for better hours and wants to transition over to my chronic unit."

"I'll gladly do it, Christy," I said, "but I'm only scheduled to be here for a few more days. Do you think that will be enough time?"

"I think so. She only needs to learn the basic day-to-day operation of the chronic unit and the differences in the paperwork."

"It's not a problem at all," I assured her. "When will you be sending her over?"

"I'd like her to start immediately, if that works for you. She's really sharp, so I don't think it will take too long for her to pick it up."

"I'm happy to do it, Christy."

"Thank you, Kenny. I'll let her know that you'll be expecting her."

"Oh, I almost forgot. What's her name?"

"Yeah, I guess you might need to know who's showing up in your clinic." she laughed. "Her name is Cara Willis."

As we both continued laughing, I said, "I'm guessing that we would have figured it out when she shows up, but this way I can let the staff know who's coming."

"Yeah, that's a good idea," she said, still chuckling at the oversight. "You never know who might show up in your clinic these days."

"You have a good point," I replied.

"Thank you again for doing this, Kenny. I really appreciate you."

"It's my pleasure, Christy. I'll never forget that it was you who gave me my start in dialysis."

We wrapped up our conversation, and I informed the staff that a nurse named Cara Willis would be training in our facility beginning next week.

At that time, I had no way of knowing just how much my life was about to change because of a last-minute decision to train a nurse as a favor to Christy. In retrospect, I've often wondered how different my life might have been had I started teaching dialysis only a few days sooner and not been available to train Cara.

On My Way Out

When I entered the facility on my next scheduled work day, I encountered the nurse Christy asked me to train. She had arrived early and was nervously awaiting my arrival. Matthew, the best dialysis tech at the facility, later told me that she kept asking, "Are you sure the charge nurse is coming?"Matthew said he had to keep reassuring her that I would be there and that I would be on time. I guess she expected me to arrive as early as she did, but arriving by 0500 hours was early enough for me. And besides, I knew that I would be the only one still working in the facility at the end of the day. We had a system, and it worked very well, even if it did make her a little nervous on her first day of training.

Because I didn't know Cara, nor had I even heard of her before Christy told me her name, I hadn't given much thought to who would be showing up. But if I had, I can assure you that I wouldn't have expected her to look the way she did. Cara was tall, thin, and even though she was wearing baggy scrubs, she was beautiful.

"You must be Cara," I said.

"Yes," she said.

I reached out to shake her hand.

"Hi, I'm Kenny."

She extended her hand, and we gently shook hands. I quickly noticed that she appeared to be very shy and unbelievably soft-spoken. In fact, over the next few days that we worked together, I would often have to say, "I'm sorry, say again?"

On the first day of her training, when it was time to take our lunch break, I noticed that she didn't appear to have anything to eat.

"Did you bring anything for lunch?" I asked.

"No," she replied.

"Well, this is your lucky day. I brought leftover chicken fajitas from Alfredo's. It's my favorite restaurant, and I have a lot more than I can eat. Would you like to share it with me?" I offered.

"Okay, thank you," she replied.

I have to admit that I was pleasantly surprised when she agreed to share my lunch. She was so shy that I thought she would decline my offer. This would be our first time to share a meal from Alfredo's, and it wouldn't be our last.

Over lunch, we began talking about work and the career change she was making. Although I had never worked in an acute dialysis unit, I was aware of the long hours and call rotation that came with the job. After years of working in that environment, I definitely understood why she wanted to move over to a chronic unit. The hours in the chronic units could be long sometimes, and you worked every other Saturday, but you always knew your schedule in advance and you were never on call. Of course, there was a lot more money to be made working in the acute setting. I guess it's like everything else in life—you just have to decide what works best for you at the time.

Over the next few days of training for Cara, I brought up the teaching position in the Education Department.

"I'm not sure if you're aware of the teaching position that opened up a while back, but I'm the one who Marsha hired to fill it," I explained.

"Congratulations," Cara said.

"I'm actually on my way out of here. In fact, if Christy had called a few days later, we wouldn't have met," I joked.

When I spoke those words, they didn't mean much to me. But lately, I've thought so much about everything that happened during those few days.

I'm not sure if it was because she realized that our time was coming to an end, or if she just began to feel more comfortable with me. Whatever the reason, Cara began to open up a little more about her desire to work in the Education Department. She even shared with me that she had actually applied for one of the teaching positions a few years earlier and that an offer had been presented to her. However, before she made the transition out of the acute unit, something had gone wrong and the offer was rescinded. When I asked her what had happened, she explained that she had spoken up during a meeting with Don, the current regional vice president, and it had made him angry. Shortly after the meeting, she was notified that she would not be moving into the teaching position. Because I was about to begin teaching dialysis, and I indirectly worked for Don, I felt a little awkward and unsure of what to say.

"I'm sorry to hear that," I said.

I had only met Don a couple of times at that point and, to be honest, I was still a little intimidated by him. He was a registered nurse who only possessed an associate degree, yet he had climbed his way up into a regional vice president position. He was tall, nice looking, appeared to take good care of himself, and although he was very polite, he had a level of confidence that could be intimidating to most everyone. And, because I had just learned that he may also be vindictive, I decided to keep quiet.

I knew that I didn't want to say the wrong thing and jeopardize my position in the Education Department, or for that matter any position within the company, so I tried to be encouraging without saying anything that could come back to bite me.

"It's been a few years, so maybe the situation has changed by now. And it's my understanding that another position will be opening up in the near future," I explained.

"There's going to be another teaching position opening up in Education?" she asked, slightly perking up.

"Yes, Marsha mentioned it to me during my interview. I don't know when it will be posted, but you might want to keep an eye out for it."

"I don't always hear about the positions when they get posted. If you don't mind, will you let me know if you hear anything about it opening up?" she asked.

"I don't mind at all," I said. "When it comes up, I'll call you at Saints just to make sure that you've heard about it."

"Would it be okay if I give you my cell phone number?" she asked. "I'd rather not let anyone know that I might be applying for another position."

Maybe it was at that moment that I should have put more thought into what I was doing, but it all seemed so innocent to me at the time. And believing that she had unfairly missed out on a teaching position in the past somehow justified my willingness to help her. But there was something else going on, too. Something about her made me feel so comfortable when I was near her. She seemed so innocent and pure, like nothing that I had ever experienced before, nor have I experienced it since. Even now, twenty years later, I still can't explain why I felt such a compelling need to help her. Regardless of the reasons, I agreed to notify her when the position opened up.

"If you don't mind handing out your cell phone number to me, I'll gladly call you." I smirked, attempting to make a joke. I'm not sure she actually got the joke, but she gave me her cell phone number.

Blacklisted

It had been a few months since I began teaching in the Education Department and since I had seen or spoken with Cara. The house that Lorrie and I were building was well under way, and it wouldn't be much longer before we could move in. This was also about the same time that Marsha told me that she was going to post the new opening for another dialysis instructor. Keeping my word to Cara, I reached out to let her know that the teaching position was about to be posted. I thought I would be able to hear the excitement in her voice, indicating that she was still interested in applying for the position, but I didn't. In fact, I had to ask her if she was still interested. She said that she was, and then she asked me, "Will you call me when it actually posts? I'm just not sure that it will make it over to our unit."

"Yeah, I'll touch base as soon as I hear about it," I replied. "I think it should be out within a few days, but I'll definitely let you know for sure."

"Thank you."

We wrapped up the call, and I returned to work.

Within a few days, Marsha informed me that the position had officially been posted. I once again followed up with Cara, who appeared to be pleased to hear from me this time. I couldn't really tell from her soft-spoken voice, but it did come across in the words that she chose.

Although it had taken several months from when I first learned about the opportunity to work as a dialysis instructor, things had begun moving pretty quickly by this time. Cara had submitted her application and was patiently waiting to hear back from Marsha.

After the application deadline had passed, Marsha screened the applicants and then discussed them in detail with me, asking for my input. Together, we selected the top candidates, then she called each of them in for their initial interview. I was able to ensure that Cara had successfully made it past the first round of cuts, but now it was up to her to interview well.

I wish I could explain why I did what I did next, but I honestly can't. That being said, one evening, a few days before her interview with Marsha, I called Cara to explain what she could expect during the interview and offered her some advice that would help her be better prepared. I asked her to keep my call confidential, which she agreed to do.

Cara was surprised and grateful for my willingness to help her, but she was also curious as to why I was helping her. I explained that I believed she was treated unfairly by Don and just wanted to help correct what I saw as an injustice. She accepted my answer, and we didn't discuss the matter again.

The reason I gave Cara was true, but to this day I am still uncertain as to why I was so willing to help her. It was also the same reason that I gave Lorrie when she asked why I was trying to help someone I didn't know very well. And although Lorrie may have accepted my answer, I am certain she was suspicious of my decision.

After Marsha interviewed the selected candidates, she briefed me, sharing her thoughts about each of the applicants. I had only been teaching dialysis for a few months, but Marsha had already told me more than once that she was very happy with my performance and grateful I was the one she had selected for the position. It was nice to receive positive feedback about my performance, but it was still too early to tell if her confidence in me would be enough to ensure that Cara got the job. Marsha had allowed me to make suggestions about the initial applicants, but I didn't know how much more input I would be allowed to offer. So, although I was able to ensure that Cara got called in for an initial interview, I wasn't sure how the rest of it was going to play out.

Marsha and I discussed all the applicants and then narrowed them down to the top three, who would be called back in for a second interview. And, as it turned out, I was able to make sure that Cara was still in the running.

I called Cara prior to her interview to let her know that Linda, not Marsha, would be conducting the second round of interviews. This was extremely important information because Linda was the person who developed the original training program for the Education Department, and she would be looking for specific attributes in an applicant. And now, I was able to ensure that Cara would be the only one of the three applicants who would have an advantage when she came in for her second interview. It was also fortunate that I had gotten to know Linda over the past few months and had a pretty good idea of the qualifications she would be seeking in an applicant. I shared all this information with Cara and wished her the best.

Linda conducted the interviews and then she, Marsha, and I met to discuss the applicants. To my surprise, Cara wasn't Linda's first choice. However, she did say that she believed all the candidates were qualified and would be capable of performing the training.

When Linda left the room, I voiced my opinion to Marsha, explaining that I thought Cara's acute dialysis experience would be a great asset to go along with my background and experience in education and chronic dialysis. I further explained that together we would be able to offer the students the best-case scenario. Marsha wasn't convinced and wanted to take some time to think about it. I tried to hide my personal feelings, acting as if it were no big deal, and then I asked her to please keep me posted, which she assured me that she would do. After only a few days she informed me that she was going to offer the position to Cara.

Before a decision was made to offer the position to Cara, just shortly after meeting with Linda and Marsha to discuss the applicants, Linda approached me and wanted to speak privately with me.

I was a little taken aback when she told me that Cara had been blacklisted by Don and she didn't know how he would react should Cara be selected for the position. I explained that although I didn't know Cara very well and didn't know that she had been blacklisted, I did have an opportunity to briefly work with her when Christy asked me to train her for the chronic unit. I shared with Linda that when Cara learned that I was moving to the Education Department, she told me what had happened to her regarding Don. I further explained that I didn't think it was fair for a qualified nurse to be excluded from a position because she spoke up during a meeting and upset the regional vice president.

To conclude our conversation, Linda said that she understood my rationale and agreed not to say anything to Marsha. I thanked her, and although we continued working together over the next several years, we never discussed the subject again. The only time it ever came up again was a few months later, when Don was in town for a meeting and stopped by the Education Department to speak with Marsha.

After their meeting concluded, Don came into the classroom to say hello to the new employees attending class. When he was finished, he briefly spoke with me and then turned to Cara.

"I see you finally made it into Education. How do you like it?" he asked her.

"I really like it," she replied.

"Good for you," he said before turning to say goodbye to all of us before he exited the room.

Don didn't know it, but because Linda told me about Cara being blacklisted, I knew what he had just done to Cara, and the message was loud and clear. I later asked her if she understood what he had done and she acknowledged that she did.

Friendship

As Cara and I spent more time working together, a close friendship began developing, and for the first time in years I was truly looking forward to going to work each day. Because our positions in Education with Fresenius required us to visit all the facilities in the state of Oklahoma, we spent a lot of time traveling together. Thus, we also began sharing personal details about our lives.

I learned that Cara had not only never been married, but she had never seriously dated anyone outside of a high school boyfriend. The few dates she did have usually didn't lead to a follow-up date. I have to admit that I was a little puzzled by this information. After all, she was so beautiful that I couldn't imagine guys not lining up to date her. She explained that because of her work schedule, she just didn't find the time to date. She said that she always wanted to be married and have children, but that at this point in her life, she couldn't imagine either of those things happening.

The most interesting discovery came as we were driving back to the office from lunch one day. We were discussing our childhood when she mentioned that she had attended Prairie Queen Elementary School.

"Are you serious?" I asked. "I actually attended school there for a year or so."

"I thought you were from Missouri," she said, surprised.

"I am, but we lived in Oklahoma until I was almost fourteen. I attended high school in Missouri, but then I moved back to Oklahoma in 1981."

We were both very surprised to learn this information, but it was about to get a lot more interesting.

"I still have my baseball uniform and a trophy with my name engraved on it from when I played for Prairie Queen," I told her. "I'll bring it to work and show you."

"When did you graduate high school?" she asked.

"I graduated in 1976. When did you graduate?"

"In 1976," she slowly answered, as if analyzing the situation and trying to understand what was happening.

"Okay, I know that it's not polite to ask a woman how old she is," I started, "but I am really curious. How old are you?"

When she told me her age and that her birthday was the following month, I couldn't believe what I was hearing.

"I'm the same age, which means that you, too, graduated high school when you were seventeen. Is that right?" I asked.

"Yes," she said, still confused.

The biggest shock came to both of us when we realized that our birth dates are almost identical. My birthday is ten days before hers, and both of our birth dates have three eights in them. In fact, seven of the eight digits in our birth dates are identical, with only one digit being different.

All these new discoveries were both exciting and a little creepy. I had never met anyone with whom I had so much in common, yet I barely knew her. It was like we were long-lost friends, and the universe was bringing us back together for some reason.

The rest of the day was a little strange to both of us as we tried to make sense of it all. We must have asked each other a million questions that afternoon. And each answer was like another piece of some cosmic puzzle that we were slowly putting together.

If Cara had any doubts about all of this new information that was coming to light, they all dissipated when I brought in my old baseball uniform and trophy to work. I could tell by the look on her face and the tone of her voice when she took the uniform from me and held it up to look it over. It was obvious that seeing the name of the school on this uniform stirred up some childhood memories in her. She handed it back to me, took the trophy from my hand and looked at it, reading the inscription out loud.

"Prairie Queen Schooners, Pee-Wee 2, 1969, Kenny Goodwin."

I thought she was going to start crying as she stared at it. And, if I'm being totally honest with myself, it stirred up some strange emotions in me, too.

The universe may have brought us together for some yet-unknown reason, but one thing I did know for sure is that we were developing a true friendship. And, as much as I enjoyed working with her, it now seemed like she was really enjoying working with me, too.

A few weeks later, Cara brought in some scotcharoos she had made the night before. It was my first time trying them, and I was hooked. Maybe it was the sugar high from all the chocolate and butterscotch, but I was becoming very fond of Cara and the friendship that had developed so quickly between us. Although I was seriously beginning to believe that Cara and I had a cosmic connection, I can honestly say that what I was feeling for her at that time was truly just friendship and nothing more.

Moving Day

The house was finished, and Lorrie and I were finally moving in. It was my first new home, and the largest house I would ever live in. We didn't realize it at the time, but we would soon learn that we had gone way overboard on the size of it. The house was a little over thirty-seven hundred square feet in size, which often felt like we were living in a small hotel. And it would soon feel much bigger to me.

One of the reasons for building a home so large was to accommodate Lorrie's mother, Sue, who was living in a care facility that specialized in patients suffering from dementia. Therefore, the majority of the lower level of our house was also wheelchair accessible, including a specially designed shower located just off of a second master bedroom.

After placing Sue in the facility, which was very expensive, Lorrie had really struggled with the decision. So, we came up with a plan to build a new home that would accommodate her mother's needs, allowing her to live with us. The plan also included Lorrie cutting down her hours at the dental office to three days a week so she could be at home Friday through Monday. I was going to continue working full time, but I would be home during the evenings and weekends and could help out her mother and give Lorrie a break.

We hired a caregiver to stay at our home with Sue during the daytime Tuesday through Thursday. The caregiver was a retired lady who had experience working with dementia patients. She didn't need the job, but she was looking for something to do on a part-time basis.

We knew these changes wouldn't be easy, but we thought that, given enough time, we would all adapt and make the best of it.

Lorrie and I took some time off from work so we could supervise the movers and get as settled in as we possibly could before bringing Sue home. Everything seemed to be going as well as could be expected, considering all the changes we were making.

After the movers brought in everything from our house in town, we put things away and got ready to get Sue and introduce her to her new home. We knew that bringing Sue into a new environment would be the most difficult part of our plan, but we had done our best to get prepared.

When it was time to bring Sue home, we invited Lorrie's sister Evon and her husband, Lloyd. We knew we could use all the help we could get, and they wanted to see how Sue handled the initial move. I wish I could say that it went as smoothly as the first part of our plan, but it didn't. As expected, Sue was confused and didn't understand why she couldn't return to the facility. She even tried bargaining with us, saying that she could come over each day and go home each night.

I understand that most humans don't like change, but I can assure you that it's much worse for most dementia patients. However, we had to remind ourselves that when we placed Sue into the facility, she constantly asked if she could come live with us. Lloyd and Evon said she also made the same request to them every time they visited her at the facility. We understood that her brain was no longer functioning properly, but we all truly believed that she would be happy to be around Lorrie all the time. After all, Lorrie was the youngest of her three children, her baby, and the two of them had always been very close.

We all took deep breaths and gave Sue some time to acclimate to her new environment. Lorrie and I would be at home for the first few days before I returned to work the following Monday. Lorrie had taken off an additional week to be with her mother and spent a couple of those days introducing Sue to her caregiver.

When I was a young man, an older coworker once told me, "A bad plan is better than no plan because you can always modify a bad plan."

I really liked the saying and even passed it along to my kids. After all, I've made several plans throughout my life that had to be modified, so I agreed that a plan had to be better than no plan. However, this would be the first time that I questioned his theory. I'm still not sure whether having a plan made any difference.

I returned to work on Monday, and Lorrie spent her first day alone with her mother. I remember calling a couple of times to see how they were doing, and everything seemed to be going well. When I returned home later that day, I learned that both Lorrie and Sue had a great day. I had no way of knowing what was about to happen only one day later.

The following morning, I went to work as Lorrie prepared to spend one more day alone with her mother before the caregiver arrived the next day. The morning was unremarkable and fairly routine. Then, upon returning from lunch, I received a call from Lorrie. I could tell something was wrong. Her voice was quivering when she said, "I don't know if I can do this."

"Did something happen to you or your mom?" I asked.

"No, I'm just not sure if I can stay home alone with her every day. It's a lot more than I thought it would be," she admitted.

"It's okay, Lorrie. We'll figure something out, but can we talk about it when I get home tonight?" I asked her.

"Yes, but I'm telling you that I don't think I can do this," she reiterated.

"It's okay. We'll talk about it tonight."

After we said our goodbyes, I got off the phone and just sat quietly for a moment. Cara and I weren't teaching class that week, so she was in my office for additional training and heard my end of the conversation.

"Is everything okay?" Cara asked.

"I don't know," I replied. "That was Lorrie. She doesn't think that she can stay home with her mother."

"I'm sorry," she said. "When you told me what you were planning to do, I was wondering if it might be too hard on her. We went through a similar situation with my grandmother before placing her in a facility, and it was really hard on my mother."

"I knew it would be hard, but I really thought we could make it work. It's the only reason we built a house so big. Now, I don't know what we're going to do."

"I really am sorry. I hope you guys can get it figured out," she said.

"Thank you, Cara."

We returned to work, and I did my best to focus on the task at hand, but the entire rest of the day I struggled to think about anything other than the new development that I would be dealing with later that day.

When I came home that evening, Lorrie and I tried talking about the situation but quickly realized that it wouldn't be possible until Sue had gone to bed. After Sue was down for the evening, Lorrie and I stayed up for hours discussing our options, but none of them seemed very good. After all, we now owned two houses, and taking Sue back to the facility would mean another added expense.

Before going to bed, we agreed to wait and see how well Sue did with the caregiver the following day. We also decided to be upfront with her regarding the situation just in case we did have to take Sue back to the facility. We would also need to reach out to the facility to see if Sue's room was still available. I asked Lorrie not to discuss anything with Evon until we knew for sure what we were doing. I couldn't see a reason for upsetting Evon and Lloyd until a final decision had been made. It was going to be a tough conversation to have with them.

Before leaving for work the next morning, I told Lorrie that I would support her decision and reassured her that we would find a way to make it work. In retrospect, I guess I already knew what decision had been made. We were just going through the motions at that point.

Therefore, it came as no surprise to me when I returned home later that afternoon and the wheels were already in motion.

Lorrie had called the facility where Sue was previously staying, and they were preparing for her return later that evening. Lorrie also informed Evon and the caregiver of our decision. She followed up with the dental office and secured her return to a full-time position beginning the following week. She had truly accomplished a lot that day. Now, we just needed to decide where we were going to live and then get the other house listed on the market.

Spoken Words

Lorrie and I decided to stay in the new home and sell the smaller one in town. A smaller home meant a smaller price, and we believed it would sell much quicker. Although the new home was designed with Lorrie's mom in mind, it also included a lot of other extras like a three-car garage, a storm shelter, a large workshop for storing our tractor and other mowing equipment, and a large movie room upstairs. All these things we could enjoy as a family, especially when the kids were staying with us. Therefore, it seemed like a waste to build something so beautiful and just walk away without the opportunity to enjoy it.

As Lorrie and I tried to settle into our new home and get the other home ready to sell, I began turning to Cara more often than Lorrie to discuss my feelings. Maybe the stress of everything I had gone through was partially to blame. I knew that I shouldn't be discussing so much personal information with her, but she had become much more than just a coworker to me. I now saw her as a close friend, and she had a way of making me feel safe when I confided in her.

If I had been a little more sensitive to the situation, I would have realized that Lorrie was beginning to feel uneasy about my relationship with Cara. Yet, no matter how many times I tried to explain that Cara was nothing more than a coworker and a friend, Lorrie wasn't buying it. Maybe Lorrie had that gut feeling we all get at times. Or maybe she was just fearful that I would develop deeper feelings for Cara. Whatever her reasons, I now know that she saw something I couldn't see at the time.

Cara and I had to travel to Woodward, Oklahoma, to train the employees in one of our chronic units. Woodward was about a three-hour drive from our offices in south Oklahoma City, which meant we had a lot of time to talk.

It was during the drive home that something happened that I still can't explain. For some unknown reason, I opened up to Cara and told her that I had developed feelings for her. I continued to share with her, saying my feelings went way beyond anything physical and that I hadn't planned on it happening. I admitted that I was struggling to understand all of it myself.

To this day, I still remember feeling so conflicted. On one hand, I knew that saying anything to her would be wrong. But I also remember thinking that if I didn't say anything, I could be missing out on the one opportunity in my life to be with someone that the universe had chosen. And unfortunately, that little voice wasn't saying anything at all that day.

I could tell she was taken by surprise. It became deathly quiet in the vehicle. She didn't respond to my comments and just stared straight ahead out the windshield. Then, my mind started spinning as I asked myself why I had said anything to her. If she told Marsha when we returned to the office, this would be the end of my career with Fresenius. Not to mention that I would soon be getting divorced when Lorrie learned about what I had said to Cara. At the very least, I had probably just destroyed a great friendship. What in the hell was I thinking?

I tried changing the subject, and Cara did her best to pretend I hadn't said anything, but we both knew what had just happened. It was an awkward feeling that filled the vehicle the entire trip back to the office. Now, I would have to wait and see if Cara said anything to Marsha.

Normal work hours were over when we arrived at the office, so we put away the training material, locked up, and headed home for the evening. I was still a little concerned about what I had said and whether Cara would mention it to Marsha, but strangely, I had calmed down a bit. Cara and I had become very close friends, and although I had crossed the line this time, I just didn't believe that she would say anything to Marsha. Maybe it was just wishful thinking on my part, but I chose to believe that she would tell me I was out of line and not to do it again, and that would be the end of it.

When I arrived at work the next morning, Cara and Marsha had already arrived, and neither of them appeared to be upset. At least the morning was off to a good start. I could only hope the rest of the day would be as uneventful.

Cara and I pulled out the work-sheets from the previous day's training and began entering in the data. Cara acted as if nothing happened the day before, and we went through the rest of that day without it ever coming up. I was a little surprised that she didn't at least tell me not to ever say anything like that again. I had even prepared an apology in case she did bring it up, but, thankfully, I didn't need it that day.

The next day started out as usual, and I continued with Cara's training. Cara had several years of acute dialysis experience, but very little chronic experience and even less computer experience. Therefore, much of the training I gave her included the use of various software applications. Fortunately, I had a lot of experience in this area, which meant I could help make her job a lot easier. And I really wanted her to succeed as an educator.

After our lunch break, we continued with the training. We were in my office going over the material when a life-changing moment occurred. I was sitting slightly off to one side so that Cara could position her chair on my left side. Because my desk was in a large "U" shape, there wasn't enough room for our chairs to be side-by-side.

Cara caught me completely off-guard with her words.

"Did you mean what you said the other day, or was it just a bunch of crap?" she softly asked.

I stopped what I was doing on the computer and turned to look directly into her eyes.

"Yes, I meant every word that I said," I replied, "and I still feel the same today."

A moment passed in silence as we just looked at each other.

"Why are you asking?" I finally asked.

"I was just curious."

"You were just curious?" I repeated.

"I feel the same way about you," she said. "But I didn't want to say anything until I knew if you really meant what you said."

"I'm being very sincere, Cara," I told her. "I've actually had feelings for you for a while now, but I was afraid to say anything." There was another long pause before I continued.

"I can't explain why I feel this way about you, but I can tell you that I've never experienced anything like this before." I remember feeling like I was stumbling with my words. Then, she softly placed her hand on top of mine and ever-so-gently wrapped her fingers around my fingers.

"I've never felt like this before, either," she told me.

I know how absurd this must sound to others, but at that moment I felt like I had just connected with my soulmate. Even now, over twenty years later, I have never experienced that feeling again except with Cara. I know that our conversation only lasted a few minutes but, while she was holding my hand, I felt like I had experienced a lifetime of cosmic energy.

She let go of my hand and smiled at me, and just like nothing had been said, we continued with the training. But from that moment forward, nothing would ever be the same in my life again.

I was smiling on the inside the entire rest of the day. Every time I looked at her, I could tell that the world had changed for her, too. I had no idea where all of this was going, but my life was definitely headed down a different path than the one it was on when I awoke that morning.

Some time later, I was scheduled to be in Tulsa for a week, performing CPR training for the employees in one of our chronic units. Cara would be staying behind and teaching dialysis to a class of newly-hired nurses. I desperately wanted her to travel to Tulsa with me, but it just wasn't possible. I suggested that she drive up after work one evening so we could go out for dinner together. The drive was only about an hour and a half, which meant that we would have enough time for dinner and for her to get some sleep after returning home. Up to this point, we had only been able to go out for lunch together, which we did several days a week. This would be our first dinner together. She said that she would think about it, but I could tell she wasn't convinced it was a good idea. I knew that it was a long shot, but I wasn't going to give up until she made her final decision.

The First Kiss

By the time I left for Tulsa on Sunday evening, Cara still hadn't committed to driving up one evening for dinner. She did, however, assure me that she was still thinking about it, though I wasn't convinced that she was putting too much thought into it. I think she sincerely wanted to spend an evening together, but I believe the hour and a half drive each way was the biggest hurdle for her to overcome. I would later learn that Cara requires at least eight or nine hours of sleep a night to feel rested the following day. I often forget that I belong to the small group of people who only require five to six hours of sleep a night.

A couple of days later, after some late-evening phone conversations, Cara finally decided to drive up to Tulsa so we could spend an evening together. I was excited to finally have an opportunity to go out for dinner with her, so I began researching restaurants close to the hotel where I was staying. Cara had previously lived in Tulsa and was very familiar with the area, so I was going to ask her to choose for us when she arrived. However, I was caught off guard when she entered my hotel room and immediately said that she didn't really want to go out to eat.

"I thought that was the reason you drove up to Tulsa," I said, confused.

"I'm just not in the mood to go out for dinner," she replied.

"It's not a problem at all. Do you want to go pick up something and bring it back to the hotel?"

"Go ahead, if you want something to eat, but I really don't feel like eating right now," she told me.

"I'm good," I said. "I'm just grateful that you decided to drive up for the evening."

"I can only stay for a while," she said.

"I understand. You let me know when you need to leave."

We sat down on the edge of the bed and made small talk for a while. I could tell that she was uncomfortable in this situation, and since I'm being honest, I was feeling a little uncomfortable, too. I was so glad to see Cara outside of work, but I hadn't forgotten that I was still married. And regardless of how strained my marriage was at that point, it was no excuse for the decisions I had been making lately. The truth is, I'm not sure why I made so many of the choices that I made. It was truly a very conflicting time for me and I guess I didn't handle it very well. I knew that I didn't want to hurt Lorrie but, for the first time in my lifetime, I had met someone who made me rethink everything about my life. I had developed feelings for Cara like I had never experienced before, and I didn't know how to deal with the situation.

I stood up and turned to face Cara. I offered my hand for her to take, and she reached out and placed her hand in mine. I then took a step back and gently pulled her up. When she stood up, I said, "Let me show you something." Still holding her hand, I walked over to the windows.

"I want to share this view with you," I told her.

"It's beautiful," she said.

"I always try to get a room up high with a great view," I told her and asked, "Are you okay with being up on one of the higher floors?"

"Yes, I love having a view like this," she answered.

"It's so peaceful to me, especially late at night or early in the morning," I explained.

"It is."

Still holding her hand, I slowly turned away from the window and walked back to the bed. I then got on the bed, laid down and said,

"I promise to not make you feel any more uncomfortable than you're already feeling. I just want to lie next to you and talk for a while."

I know it probably sounds like a typical line to get someone in bed, but I truly had no intention of making her feel uncomfortable or putting her in a position where she had to tell me to stop. And I could tell that she believed me when she crawled onto the bed and lay down next to me. We lay there in silence, looking into each other's eyes for a few minutes before we started with the small talk again. I remember having a smile on my face and thinking that she probably thought I was so goofy.

"What's so funny?" she asked.

"I feel like a little kid right now," I laughed. "I know it's probably stupid, but I can't stop smiling."

"It's not stupid," she reassured me. "I feel happy, too. I just don't show my feelings like you do."

"Thank you, Cara."

I don't recall how long we talked, or even what we talked about. I just remember feeling so peaceful in her presence. She was so beautiful, so soft-spoken and so gentle; a true girly-girl, which was something I had never experienced before. I was a hyper kid, and that carried over into my adult life. I had learned to occasionally keep it under control, but mostly I was just hyper. And the worst part of it for me was how loud I could get when I was excited, even when the excitement was for something wonderful. It's just how I'm wired. I have to work really hard at not being too loud, but it's mostly a losing battle.

It was getting late, and I knew that she would need to be leaving soon if she hoped to get any sleep that night. I'm still not sure where I found the courage (maybe it was the fear of her leaving before I finally got up the nerve to ask her the question), but I finally asked her, "How long are you going to make me wait before I can kiss you?"

I would later find out that she was actually hoping I would kiss her that night. But that's not something I would have done without her permission. Yes, I know it's old fashioned and a little weird, but it's just who I am. Not to mention that I'd never been with anyone so sweet and precious in my life. I didn't know women like Cara actually existed, other than in romantic-comedy movies. You know the type, the sweet, shy, quiet, beautiful girl next door.

Although it took her a little by surprise when I finally got the words out, she immediately leaned in, softly touched the side of my face and kissed me. I may forget many things as I grow old, but I'll never forget that first kiss with Cara. It was more than just a kiss. It was the beginning of something special for both of us. And for the first time, I truly wanted to spend the rest of my life with someone.

After lying next to each other for some time, we eventually got up and walked back to look out the window. We held on to each other, and I'd never felt so close to another human being.

"So, what happens now?" Cara asked.

"I don't know, but I know that I want to be with you, Cara," I said.

"I want to be with you, too, Kenny." She hugged me a little tighter.

"I guess I need to talk to Lorrie when I get home," I said.

"What are you going to tell her?"

"I'm going to be honest and tell her that I've developed feelings for you."

"Do you think that's a good idea?" she asked.

"I've been downplaying my feelings for you for quite a while, and I don't want to lie to her anymore. I know she's not going to take it well, but I need to be honest with her."

"I wish you would leave me out of it," she admitted.

"I don't think it matters what I tell her, she'll know I'm leaving her for you. But I'll make sure and put the blame all on me."

It was getting late and I didn't want her to leave, so I suggested that she spend the night, get up early and drive back in the morning. This would allow her to get a few hours of sleep before driving back to Oklahoma City. I gave her my word that I wouldn't try taking our relationship any further than it had already gone. She agreed to stay. I kept my word to her, and we even slept on top of the covers with our clothes on, covered up with an extra blanket. This was truly a first for me in so many ways.

We slept for a few hours, and in the morning, I walked her down to her car.

"Please call me when you get home," I said. "And if you have any problems along the way, call me immediately. Or if you just want to talk while you're driving home, I'll gladly stay on the phone with you until you get home."

"I'll be okay," she reassured me. "But I'll call you when I get home or if I need anything."

"Okay. Please drive safely."

"I will," she said, smiling at me.

We said our goodbyes, and she headed home. I went back to the room and lay down, but I was too amped up to go back to sleep. My head was spinning, but as excited as I was about starting a new relationship with Cara, I knew it was going to break Lorrie's heart.

The Red Dress

No matter how many times I played the scenario over in my mind, I couldn't come up with a way to tell Lorrie the truth without hurting her. She had done nothing wrong, and she didn't deserve the pain this was about to inflict upon her. The worst part was that I knew exactly the kind of pain this was going to cause her. After all, it was the same pain that I experienced when Vonda filed for a divorce.

I tried to mitigate what I was doing by telling myself that Lorrie had surprised Tommy when she divorced him and broke his heart. But I knew that no matter what had happened in her past relationship, it didn't change the fact that I was about to change the course of both of our lives, and this time it was all on me.

When I headed home from Tulsa at the end of the week, I was feeling sick. My stomach was upset from all the dread, and I was popping antacids like they were gumdrops. I even began second-guessing my decision to leave Lorrie. After all, how well did I really know Cara? I knew we'd spent a lot of time together over the past several months, but we'd never dated. Hell, we hadn't even had sex at that point. We'd kissed, and that was it. Did I want to throw away a marriage for someone I didn't really know?

No matter how many questions I asked myself, the answer was always the same. I can't explain it, but there was something so special about Cara, that I was willing to undo my entire life to be with her. I know it wouldn't have made sense to anyone else, but for some strange, cosmic reason, it made sense to me. I truly believed that we shared something special and that the stars were finally lining up in my favor.

In 1980, Bob Seger released a song called "Against the Wind," which contained the line, "Wish I didn't know now what I didn't know then." Fourteen years later, in 1994, Toby Keith released an entire song about the same line, and it became one of his biggest hits. As a huge fan of both artists, I was very familiar with the line, and I still catch myself saying it to this day. The entire weekend after I returned home from Tulsa, I couldn't get it out of my head. I knew that the moment I told Lorrie I wanted a divorce, we could never go back to a time when she hadn't heard me say those words. It was for this reason that I put it off as long as I could and didn't say anything to her until Sunday afternoon.

Unfortunately, it went as badly as it possibly could have gone. We stayed up most of the night talking. And just as I had done when Vonda broke the news to me, Lorrie cried until she couldn't cry anymore.

Although I did my best to keep Cara's name out of the conversation, Lorrie knew the reason I was asking for a divorce. She threatened to call Cara numerous times throughout the night. Because I had experienced some of the same feelings when Vonda and I divorced, I tried to be understanding and compassionate. However, when Lorrie threatened to contact Marsha and try to get me fired, I began losing my patience with her.

"Is this how Tommy treated you when you divorced him?" I asked.

"I didn't leave Tommy for another person," she fired back.

"No, but you did leave him for a different lifestyle. And you didn't waste any time before you started dating again," I reminded her. "So it was okay for you to divorce him, but God forbid anyone wants to make a change if it involves you."

We would argue for a while before calming down and talking about how we would proceed. Then the cycle would begin all over again. I've learned that going through a divorce can be one of the most difficult, heart-wrenching experiences in the world.

We eventually came up with a short-term plan before going to bed and trying to get some sleep. We decided that I would remain in the new house until it sold, and Lorrie would return to our home in town. We hadn't yet listed the other house on the market, but we would now need to find a real estate agent to list it. Because of the size of the house, I was concerned it wouldn't be a quick sale. I was also regretting that we had built a house so big because I would be staying in it alone. I had lived alone for years, but never in a house so big or with so few neighbors. It was definitely going to take some getting used to, and I had no idea how long it would take for the house to sell.

Because of the circumstances, Cara and I couldn't start dating and had to be mindful of our working relationship. It was one of the most difficult times of my life, and on occasion, I was concerned that Cara would get tired of waiting for the house to sell and give up on me. She assured me that she wouldn't, but there were times when she became frustrated with me.

"Why are you waiting for the house to sell before getting divorced?" she asked me one day at the office.

"Because I told Lorrie that I wouldn't file for a divorce until after the house sells," I explained.

Then, Cara caught me off guard, and for the first time in our relationship, I saw another side of her.

"Why do you let her yank you around by the nose like a little puppy dog?" she asked.

"Because she is technically still my wife," I snapped back at her.

She could tell I was becoming irritated and changed the direction of the conversation.

"I know you're doing the right thing and I'm just being selfish," she said as she reached out to hold my hand.

"Thank you, Cara." I took her hand and held it for a minute. "Hopefully, it won't be much longer before the house sells."

"It's okay. I know you're doing your best to get it sold," she reassured me.

I'm not sure if that conversation played a part, or if it was just the fact that I wouldn't divorce Lorrie before the house sold, but things were about to change in a big way.

Cara and I had an upcoming training session on some new equipment at Saint Anthony Hospital. Because the training had to be done while the patients were receiving dialysis, both Cara and I would need to be at the facility for much of the day. As it turned out, the training was scheduled on my birthday. This would end up being serendipity at its finest.

A few days before the training, we made plans to meet at the office and ride to the facility together. Although I usually drove my car when we traveled together, Cara said she wanted to drive this time. I agreed, and our plans were finalized. Before leaving for the day, I gave her a hard time about bringing scotcharoos for my birthday. She knew they had become my favorite treat and how much I was looking forward to them again.

I was already in the office the following Monday when Cara arrived carrying the scotcharoos. I know I should have made a big deal about the treats, but I was so distracted. Cara was wearing the most beautiful form-fitting red dress I had ever seen. She looked gorgeous. The dress was so classy, reaching down to just a few inches above her knees and showing off her long, tanned legs.

"I apologize for being a little distracted, but you look beautiful, Cara," I told her as I stared, unable to take my eyes off her.

"Thank you. I thought I'd surprise you on your birthday," she said seductively.

"Oh, you did! I was just hoping for the scotcharoos," I laughed.

"You got those, too."

"You know I'm going to have a hard time, pun intended, getting any work done today," I said with a big smile on my face.

"Good," she said, smiling back at me.

"Well, I guess we'd better head to the facility and get started with the training," I told her.

"I'm ready if you are."

As we walked out to her car, I couldn't stop staring at her. She looked like a model who had just stepped off the cover of Vogue Magazine. I really couldn't believe that this classy, beautiful lady was interested in me. It just didn't make any sense at times. But when thoughts about it being too good to be true entered my mind, I simply convinced myself that it was finally my turn and that my life was in perfect harmony with the universe.

After arriving at the facility, we spent the morning and early afternoon training the staff to use the new equipment. Because I wanted to finish the training and get back to the office, where the scotcharoos were waiting for me, we worked through lunch and finished up a little early. What I didn't know was that Cara had one more surprise for me that day.

We pulled out of the parking garage and Cara started taking a different route.

"Is this some devious plan to keep me away from the scotcharoos?" I asked.

"You'll see," she replied.

"If your plan is to kidnap me and take me away from this life, all you have to do is say the word," I joked.

"Don't worry, I'm just taking a little detour."

Although I had no idea where we were going, I didn't care as long as I was with her.

It didn't take long before I realized where she was going, and my mind began racing. She was driving to her house. I didn't say anything and instead decided to wait and see if this was really the plan. I didn't have to wait much longer. I was right. She pulled her car into the garage, out of view from anyone driving through the neighborhood.

When we got inside, she took my hand and walked me to her bedroom at the back of the house. It wasn't my first time inside her house or even in her bedroom. (I once connected a DVD player to the TV so she could watch movies in her bedroom.) But it was the first time that I had entered her bedroom with the real possibility of making love with her. And I have to admit that I was still wondering if this was really happening. We had talked and joked about it, and some of our kisses had been pretty intense, but we had never crossed that line until now.

Because I don't want this beautiful experience to turn into a *Fifty Shades of Grey* moment, I will only say that taking off her dress and laying it on the chair to prevent it from wrinkling was a moment that took my breath away. There's a saying that I love so much that not only did I share it with her that day, but years later, we placed a beautiful plaque with that inscription on our living room wall (where it is still hanging today). If you're not familiar with the saying, it reads, "Life is not measured by the number of breaths we take, but by the moments that take our breath away." Without going into further detail, I will say that making love with Cara for the first time also took my breath away.

On the way back to the office, I felt so close to her that I could barely contain my emotions. Although I've obviously been with other women, I had never experienced feelings like the ones I felt on that day. In every way possible, she truly was the girl next door.

Just like with our first kiss, my feelings for Cara only deepened after making love with her. And although it wasn't my first time to feel a special connection with Cara, on that day, once again, it felt like I had connected with my soulmate.

Maybe it was still just wishful thinking at that point, but I was truly starting to believe that she had followed me into this life. I had joked about it with her, and more than once I teased her about it in front of the students. But on that day, it seemed like much more than just wishful thinking. If it's possible to fall under the spell of another person, I had fallen so deeply that there was no turning back.

I'm not sure if it was Cara's red dress that did me in, or if I simply grew tired of waiting for a buyer to come along and purchase the house so that I could be with her. Regardless of the reasons, I explained to Lorrie that we needed to reassess the situation and see what we had to do to get the house sold. Lorrie agreed, and we sat down together and crunched the numbers. We decided to come up with a bottom-line figure that would get our investment back, pay the real estate agent's fee, and pay our share of the closing costs. After we came up with the new number, the real estate agent held another open house and received two offers on that very day.

The agent made it clear to potential buyers that we would not be accepting any offers that did not meet our new asking price. Fortunately, both offers met our asking price, and one of the offers was from a local real estate agent. Therefore, when we countered her offer, asking only that she waive her real estate fees, she agreed, and within a few weeks we closed on the house.

I moved what little furniture I owned into a duplex and, for the first time since meeting, Cara and I began openly dating. Now, all that was left to do was to settle up on the house that Lorrie was living in and had decided to keep for herself. We quickly agreed on a price, and then Lorrie asked a friend to draft the paperwork for the divorce.

During the final days before the divorce was finalized, Lorrie and I occasionally needed to discuss minor details regarding the paperwork. It was during one of these conversations that Lorrie shared some intimate details about Cara.

"I thought you might like to know a couple of things about your girlfriend," she said.

Thinking that she was looking to take a cheap shot at Cara in hopes of upsetting me, I told myself not to overreact to any of her comments.

"You should know she's not even a real blonde," she said smugly.

"Lorrie, you know that I could care less about someone's natural hair color," I retorted. "Vonda's a brunette, you have red hair, and Cara's hair is blonde. I'm not one of those guys who only date women with a particular hair color."

"She's also gay!" she fired back.

I slowly shook my head and smiled.

"She's not gay, Lorrie," I told her. "Why would you even say something like that?"

It was obvious to Lorrie that I didn't believe a word she was saying, and she was becoming upset.

"Well, she lived in a one-bedroom apartment with another woman for about 10 years," she explained.

"Look, I don't know where you got your information, but I'm telling you, you're wrong!" I argued.

Lorrie began explaining how she learned this information, which took me by surprise.

"I told Cara that I thought you were tracking me, but I never thought you would go that far," I replied.

I was becoming frustrated and I didn't want to argue with Lorrie, so I ended the conversation.

"Please let me know if you need anything else, so that we can get the paperwork completed," I said before I turned and walked toward the front door.

Later that day, I spoke with Cara and told her what Lorrie had said, but I didn't tell her how she obtained the information. Cara quickly explained that she was not gay and that she had lived in the apartment alone for approximately 10 years before she purchased her home. She did say that the lady who rented the apartment to her was gay but assured me that *she* was not. I was satisfied with her explanation, and that was the end of the conversation. The subject wouldn't come up again for nearly two decades.

On March 23, 2007, the divorce was finalized, and my marriage to Lorrie officially ended. If only I had known the significance that date would one day hold.

Matching Scars

During the time between Cara's "Red Dress" surprise birthday gift and finalizing my divorce with Lorrie, I was offered a position as acute service manager for the Oklahoma City metro area. I knew the job would be a big step up in the company; but that it could also be an overwhelming position. This was evident by the number of nurses who had accepted the position only to walk away within a few months. The only nurse who stayed in the position for any significant length of time was Linda, and everyone knew she was a workaholic. So, before I accepted the position, I made two requests to Todd, the area manager overseeing the unit. My first request was that I would be allowed to restructure the unit so that it would function more efficiently. My second request was regarding the salary. I knew that taking on the role of acute service manager would mean that I would be working long hours, so I asked to be hired with a higher salary. I assured Todd that he would get his money's worth out of me and that I wouldn't disappoint him. He agreed to my requests, and on June 5, 2006, I started working my new position.

One of my reasons for accepting the position had to do with Cara. I knew that if we were working in different departments, we wouldn't encounter any issues when we officially began dating. After all, there were several couples working in the company. The only rules were that the couples couldn't work together in the same unit, nor could one partner report to the other. So, accepting a new position would make it much easier for Cara and me to go public with our relationship when the time was right. And the icing on the cake was that my new office was located in the same strip mall, just two doors down from the Education Department. This meant that we could still see each other every day and have lunch together regularly.

We didn't know it at the time, but plans were already underway to relocate the Education Department into the same area as the Acute Department, which had a large training room and several vacant offices. It did take a while, but after the move, Cara's office was only two doors down from mine. It couldn't have worked out any better even if we had been in charge of the planning ourselves.

It's still difficult for me to understand everything that happened, which led me to believe that Cara and I were somehow cosmically linked. But things I took as signs from the universe continued to happen.

One day, Cara told me she had developed a small mass on the inside of her lower right knee. We both agreed that she needed to be seen by a physician, so she made an appointment. A few weeks later, when Cara returned to the office from her appointment, she told me that the physician's assistant had removed the mass and, as a precautionary measure, sent the tissue to the lab for a biopsy. He explained that it was probably not anything to be concerned about, but this way he could be certain. He then stitched her up and concluded the visit.

I didn't explain why, but I asked Cara if I could see the area where the mass had been removed. When she showed me the stitches on her leg, I said I had something to show her.

"Cara, I know this is probably not a big deal to you, but I want to show you something on the inside of my left knee," I explained. I then pulled up my pant leg and showed her the small scar on the inside of my left knee. I remember the look of disbelief on her face when she looked down at the scar and then back up at me. She stared into my eyes for a minute before saying anything.

"How did you get that scar?" she asked.

"It happened when I was eight years old. I was in a grocery store," I said. "I was carrying an eight-pack of soda in one hand and an eight-pack of empty glass bottles in my other hand. On my way to the checkout counter, the bottom of the pack with the full bottles came apart, causing the bottles of soda to hit the floor and bust open. I remember soda was spilling all over the place, and it took a few seconds before I realized that blood was running down my leg onto the floor."

"Oh my goodness," she replied.

"Thankfully, a young man working at the checkout picked me up and rushed me into a private room. Someone placed a tourniquet on my leg and then they called for an ambulance."

"Were you at the store alone?" she asked.

"No, my mom, Roger and Terri were all waiting in the car, so someone went out and got them," I explained. "Now, here's the weirdest part of this story. The ER doctor told me that he used eight stitches," I said, shaking my head in disbelief.

Not grasping the significance of that, she asked me, "Why is that the weirdest part?"

"I was eight years old, the cartons of soda were both eight packs, and I got eight stitches," I explained before asking her, "What's my birth date?"

She thought for a split second before commenting.

"Okay, that is strange."

"And now, we're going to have matching scars, but on opposite knees," I said as I smiled at her. "I'm telling you, Cara, there is something very cosmic going on with us. I can't explain it, I don't understand it, but I do believe it."

"I do get it, and I think you're right," she said.

At the time, I truly believed the universe was sending me signs, proving to me that Cara and I were cosmically linked. Now, it feels like the universe was playing a cruel joke on me.

Two Murders

There would be many events over the next several years that strengthened my belief in our cosmic relationship. But there were some events I never thought could be connected to us. It just never entered my mind, at least not for many years to come. On February 3, 2007, when one of our coworkers, Randy Glasser, was murdered, I saw it as the most horrific work-related event that had ever taken place in my life. But I didn't think it could even remotely be linked to our relationship. And if Randy had been the only coworker to have been murdered during the time that Cara and I were together, I wouldn't be sharing my story. But this was just the beginning of a long list of tragic events that would take place during our time together.

It was only a few weeks before Randy was murdered that I saw him in Dallas, Texas. Randy had transferred from Oklahoma City to Dallas to take the chief tech position, and I was visiting the clinic where he worked. We didn't have much time to catch up, so I invited him to go to lunch with a small group of us. Unfortunately, he declined, saying that he had too much work to do. I told him I understood and that we could try again next time I was in Dallas.

I would only learn about this after his death, but at the time, Randy was secretly dating the clinic manager, Wendy. I now suspect this had more to do with why he hadn't joined us for lunch than his workload. Because Wendy had recently gone through a very contentious split from her ex-boyfriend John Robert Spencer, I believe she and Randy were just trying to keep the peace. Unfortunately, Spencer would turn out to be the ex from hell, as well as a raging murderer.

Word about Randy's death had already begun spreading throughout the company when Cara and I returned to work on Monday. The gory details of the event would soon follow. As more information came to light, we learned that Wendy was staying with Randy when her ex-boyfriend broke into the house and beat Randy, who was unarmed, to death with a baseball bat. It seemed unfathomable that someone so kind could lose their life in such a violent manner, but that's exactly what happened. And there was nothing that any of us could do to change it. We all felt so helpless.

On Tuesday, February 6, 2007, Randall (Randy) Andrew Glasser was laid to rest at Resurrection Cemetery in Oklahoma City. Cara and I attended the service together, along with many of Randy's coworkers from Fresenius Medical Care. It was a very difficult day, to say the least. Sadly, there would be many more difficult days to follow before the shock of Randy's death began subsiding and our lives could find some kind of new normal.

About five months later, during the week of July 4, 2007, Cara and I went on our first vacation together. By this time, everyone who knew us was aware that we were officially a couple, and it was nice to be able to openly make plans together. It was also the first time that I would be meeting her entire family. I had met some of her family members when I attended a musical event for her niece Lauren, but I was only there for about an hour, which didn't allow me enough time to get to know everyone. This time, things would be very different.

Cara and I traveled to Pagosa Springs, Colorado, to spend an entire week with her family. Because we weren't married, we wouldn't be sharing a bedroom on this trip. Her family were all practicing Christians, and sleeping together before marriage was frowned upon. We would, however, be staying in the same cabin with adjoining bedrooms, but Cara would be sharing a room with Lauren, while I had a private room. I have to admit that it felt a little strange sleeping in separate bedrooms, but I wanted to make a good impression on her family, so I was willing to do whatever was needed to accomplish the task.

My first impression of her family was that they were all kind, generous, and very religious. I knew that Cara was raised with a strict Christian upbringing, and because of the way our relationship had begun I didn't really know what to expect from her family. Cara did, however, advise me that it would be best if I didn't mention my spiritual beliefs to anyone. She explained that her family would not understand. Cara, on the other hand, knew that I was spiritual, but not religious.

During one of our many late-night talks, I had explained to Cara that I do believe in a higher power (which is often referenced as God or the universe), spirits (also known as angels, souls, or a form of energy), and the power of prayer. However, after being a practicing Christian for many years, I had eventually made a choice not to participate in any religion. Cara assured me that she understood, and we both agreed to respect each other's beliefs. It worked for us, but it was obvious that it wouldn't work for her family.

I learned that Cara and her older sister, Gwen, were extremely close, yet Cara was not nearly as close to their older sister, Neesa. Cara was also close to Gwen's husband, Steve, but not as close to Neesa's husband, Billy. When I later asked her about the differences, she said it was because of their ages. She explained that Neesa was older and had her own bedroom, while she and Gwen shared a bedroom growing up, which made sense to me. I would later learn that there was a lot more to the family dynamics and to Cara and Gwen's relationship. If I had only known the problems Cara and I would eventually encounter because of their sibling relationship, I would have made so many different choices at the time.

It became apparent that not only Cara seemed to idolize Gwen, but the entire family appeared to put Steve and Gwen on a pedestal, constantly praising them, and never questioning their decisions. Now, in all fairness to Steve and Gwen, I agree that if you're paying for all the cabins for a week for about twenty people (which they so generously did), you should have a say in where everyone would be staying. However, I noticed that they not only decided on the sleeping arrangements, but they made most of the decisions for everyone during the entire vacation. They had a plan for every day of the week, including the days each family would be responsible for preparing meals, the days we would all eat out together, and the so-called "free" days when everyone would be on their own. As someone who is extremely detail-oriented and always tries to have a plan, I loved how they managed all of it, at least in the beginning of my relationship with Cara.

We were all having a wonderful time and I truly felt welcomed by everyone. Cara's elderly father and mother were two of the kindest people and the best Christians I'd ever had the pleasure of meeting. And then there were the nieces, nephews, in-laws, and all the kids. Steve and Gwen have one daughter, Lauren; and Billy and Neesa have three children, Michelle, Dustin, and Delana, and a handful of grandchildren. It was a little confusing the first few days as I attempted to learn everyone's names and the families to which they belonged, but even so, I couldn't believe how friendly and kind everyone was to me. They all made me feel so welcome and comfortable. But maybe if I hadn't been so enamored with Cara, I would have reminded myself of the old saying "When something seems too good to be true, it probably is." In fact, during a phone call with my mom a few days after the trip, I admitted to her that there was something I couldn't put my finger on, something that made me think of the group as being cult-like.

A few days into the vacation, I received a call from my mom. She and my dad were living in Springfield, Missouri, and she had just read in the local newspaper that Rolland Comstock had been found murdered in his home. We later learned that he had been shot at close range multiple times and that although divorced, he and ex-wife Alberta Comstock were still fighting over the mansion where Rolland was murdered. And because Rolland had two pet wolves living with him, the police knew it had to be someone the wolves were familiar with, someone they had allowed to enter the house.

Rolland was a prominent attorney and nationally recognized book collector with over fifty thousand books in his collection. He had also served as a Missouri state legislator in 1964 for Green County. But how is all this related to my story? Rolland was my brother's former father-in-law. My brother, Roger, was previously married to Rolland's daughter Sherry, and the wedding reception was held at the Comstock home. Rolland even provided a few of us attending the wedding with a personal tour of his private library, an unbelievably beautiful room in their home. I realized that day why so many people referred to the house as a mansion. It's the biggest private home that I've ever seen, owned by someone I had actually known. At the time of Rolland's death, Roger and Sherri had been divorced for many years, but learning about his murder was still shocking news to our family.

After speaking with my mom, I immediately informed Cara of the news I had just received. She was obviously surprised and had a lot of questions. I explained how this was all tied to our family and said, "I know this is probably going to sound strange, but before Randy died, I'd never personally known anyone who had been murdered. Now, five months after Randy was murdered, my brother's former father-in-law was murdered."

"That really is strange," she agreed.

"Yeah, maybe it's like that old saying about people dying in groups of three," I joked. "I sure hope that's not the case this time."

"Yeah, me too," she joked back.

We brushed it off and went about enjoying our day. That evening, we all got together to watch the fireworks put on by the town of Pagosa Springs in celebration of the Fourth of July. It was a beautiful show, and I really enjoyed spending time with Cara and her family. Thankfully, the remainder of the trip was unremarkable (at least regarding any tragedies), and I really hated to see it come to an end.

The Definition of Insanity

I'm not sure who said it, but I've often heard the phrase, "The definition of insanity is repeating the same thing over and over again and expecting a different outcome." If this statement is truly accurate, then I must be insane.

The latter half of 2007 was a busy time for us. I had reorganized the Acute Services Department, and it was running as smoothly as could be expected for a unit that's often described as "organized chaos." However, it still took up a great deal of my time. The Education Department had moved into the same area as the Acute Dialysis Department, and Cara and I were once again working in proximity to one another. Cara sold her house and moved into a duplex near the duplex I had rented after selling my and Lorrie's house. Cara and I often joked about being two doors down from each other all day and each evening.

I offered to let Cara move into my duplex with me, but she explained that her family would never understand or approve of us living together before being married. Fortunately, this was the first time that I actually wanted to be married, and I was excited about spending the rest of my life with Cara. It was a feeling I had never experienced before and that I'm convinced I will never feel again. There was something about this angelic, beautiful lady that made me push all caution aside and move forward with our relationship.

Cara knew I felt like a failure with two divorces under my belt, but she also knew that I was in love with her, which was another first for me. Yes, I cared for Vonda and Lorrie, but I'd never been in love, which is one of the reasons I was willing to bet against the odds and get married again.

The only real concern I had was about the finances. Because I lost everything during the first divorce, I told myself I would never again allow anyone to have access to my finances. Cara assured me that she understood, and we agreed to move forward with the same arrangement that Lorrie and I had during our marriage. So, with the exception of purchasing a home together and opening a joint checking account, we agreed to keep our finances separated. This had served me well with Lorrie, and it was the only way that I was willing to move forward, even with the only person I had ever fallen in love with.

I surprised Cara one Sunday when I told her that I needed to pick up something from the mall and asked her to join me. She agreed and we headed out to Quail Springs Mall. Curious, she asked me what I needed to pick up, and I jokingly told her that it was a surprise. I was sure she had no idea what I was planning.

We walked through the mall holding hands, which was another first for me. I'm not sure why, but I'd never felt comfortable holding hands with anyone before meeting Cara. And this was just one of so many firsts for us, even though we met later in life.

As we were passing by Gordon's Jewelry, I turned into the store and gently pulled her along with me. Once inside, I stopped and looked at her.

"I thought it might be a good day to start looking at rings," I said.

"Are you serious?" she cautiously asked.

"Unless you have an objection to looking," I replied. "I won't know what you like unless you show me."

It was obvious by the smile on her face that I had truly surprised her, and she was excited to start looking at rings.

It didn't take too long until she found a ring she really liked. It wasn't a typical wedding set, so it didn't come with the engagement ring or a man's wedding ring. Fortunately, the sales rep was able to match it with a ring that I liked, and it actually looked like a set that had been ordered together.

I explained to the sales rep that we had just started looking and wanted to take some time to think about it, and we left the store.

"Would you like to stop by the other jewelry store and see what they have?" I asked Cara.

"We can if you like, but I really like that ring we just looked at," she replied.

"I liked it, too," I said. "Then why don't we stop by the food court, get something to drink and talk about it."

"That sounds great," she said as she smiled her beautiful smile at me.

We stopped in the food court, purchased our drinks and sat down in a booth.

"Cara, I'll leave it up to you, but if you like that ring and this is something you really want to do, maybe we should just get them today," I suggested.

That was the closest I've ever gotten to a proposal in my life. I have never asked anyone to marry me, but to this day I regret not officially proposing to Cara. Regardless of how it would work out in the future, she deserved better than what I offered her on that day.

"Are you suggesting that we get married?" she asked me.

"Yes," I said. "If we get the rings today, you can decide how you want to proceed. Because I've been married before and this is your first marriage, I want you to decide what kind of wedding you want."

"I can tell you right now that I don't want a big church wedding," she said.

I have to admit that I was taken aback by her reply. I thought for sure that a big church wedding was exactly what she was expecting.

"What are you thinking?" I asked.

"I'd like a small wedding with only our families attending," she explained. "And I'd like to have it at Gwen's house."

"Okay, if that's what you want then I'm good with it. Do you know when you want to get married?" I asked her.

"Yes, I was thinking about March."

I didn't consider at the time just how significant the month of March had become in my life. Maybe it's just one big coincidence, but I'll never believe that's what it is, not for a second.

"Okay. I'll let you take it from here. Just let me know what I can do to help, other than stay out of the way and show up on time," I jokingly said.

We finished our drinks and returned to Gordon's to buy the rings. The rest of the day was very exciting for both of us. We spent the entire afternoon talking about where we would spend our honeymoon and where we would live afterwards.

Neither Cara nor I had ever been on a cruise, so we decided that would be a wonderful way to spend our honeymoon. It was another one of those firsts for both of us. So, for the next few weeks we spent our evenings researching cruises and excursions we thought would be exciting to do. Then, after gathering a great deal of information, we made an appointment with a travel agency and booked our trip. Now it was time to decide where we would live after returning home.

We looked at a few different neighborhoods we thought we would like to live in, and we decided that we wanted to build a new house for our first home together. Once we made the decision to build a new house, we located a neighborhood under development on the west end of town and contacted one of the builders.

Because there weren't many houses in the neighborhood, we were able to pick a lot at the very end of a road that backed up to a greenbelt. By picking this lot, no one could ever build behind us or to the south of us. Our home would be the last house on a dead-end road (yes, just like the horror movie *The Last House on the Left*). Was it was an omen that I missed?

With construction of the house underway, we decided that Cara would move into the duplex with me when we returned from our honeymoon. So, just before getting married, we moved her furniture into a storage unit, and she moved in with her sister Gwen and her family. It seemed a little strange to me, but I really wanted to please Cara and her family, and I knew it would only be for a short time. Then, we would be able to spend the rest of our lives living together and doing things our way. Or so I thought.

March 1, 2008, finally arrived. When Cara's father, Wayne, walked her into the room set up for the wedding, I couldn't believe my eyes. Cara looked stunning in her wedding dress. I was having a hard time believing that this day was finally happening. I was actually getting married to the love of my life, and she was the most beautiful soul that I had ever met. In fact, I would spend the next fifteen and a half years telling everyone that she was the best Christian that I had ever known in my life.

After the ceremony (which included saying our vows, taking photos, and signing the marriage license), followed by a small reception, we were on our way to spend one night in a beautiful hotel (courtesy of a wedding gift from Steve and Gwen) in downtown Oklahoma City before flying out the next morning to Florida, where we would board the cruise ship. If only the next day had gone as smoothly as our wedding day. But it wasn't meant to be.

We left early to arrive at the airport on time for our flight. Unfortunately, when we arrived to check in we encountered a lady behind the counter who was having a terrible morning. It was obvious she had run into some issue she couldn't handle and had to call someone multiple times for assistance. When she finally sorted it out, I politely spoke up and asked her if she would be able to check all of us in on time for our flights. She obviously didn't like my question, so I thought it would be best to remain quiet, which I did. Then, after another thirty minutes or so, she asked, "Is there anyone here that's flying to Florida?"

I raised my hand. "We're flying to Florida."

When no one else raised their hand, she said, "Then you need to come up to the counter."

"Now, ahead of these other people?" I asked.

"Yes," she demanded.

As we made our way to the front of the line, I apologized to those standing before us. Everyone was very kind and understanding.

"It looks like I'm going to have to book you on another flight," the lady informed us.

"I don't understand," I said. "We still have enough time to make our flight."

"There are no more seats available on that flight."

I protested. "How can that be? We have reserved seating on that flight."

"It looks like they overbooked the flight," she said.

At this point, Cara was about to break down, so I had to console her as I was also dealing with the lady behind the counter.

"Can you get us to Florida on time to board the cruise ship?" I asked the lady.

"What time do you board the ship?" she asked.

"We board at 4:00 p.m."

"Yes, I can get you there on time," she replied.

"Thank you," I said, biting my tongue to keep from telling her what I was really thinking at that moment.

I realize that most people would probably have seen this as an omen to our future together, but I didn't. I'm not sure why I overlooked so much, but in retrospect, I think I was so in love with Cara that I didn't want to see any negative signs.

The airline rep got us checked in on the new flight, and told us to go directly to a specific gate for immediate boarding. Cara and I had to rush through the airport terminal in order to make that flight.

After boarding the plane to Salt Lake City, Utah, we began calming down, relieved that we would arrive in Florida on time to board the ship. I was, however, frustrated that the airline overbooked the flight, and it didn't help my frustration to learn that overbooking was a very common practice with airlines.

We arrived in Salt Lake City, and it appeared that although we had gotten off to a bad start, it would all work out in the end. And then, an airline rep made an announcement that changed everything.

The airline rep announced that there was a mechanical problem with the plane we were about to board, and they were waiting on an alternate plane to arrive. Unfortunately, we did not make it to Florida on time to board the cruise ship. However, in all fairness to the airlines, they put us up in a hotel in Florida and flew us out the next day to San Juan, Puerto Rico, which was the first stop for the cruise ship. So, although we missed the first two days at sea, we had a beautiful room overlooking the Atlantic Ocean and got to spend two days sightseeing and enjoying the food in beautiful San Juan before finally boarding the cruise ship. And although we had, once again, gotten off to a rocky start, it really was all working out wonderfully.

Karma

The construction on the house was finally completed, and on July 1, 2008, Cara and I moved into our new home. Although it seemed like nothing more than a nice gesture at the time, Cara's sister Gwen and their parents were there to help oversee the move. I actually appreciated the help until I realized that Cara wouldn't decorate our house without Gwen's opinion on the placement of every single item.

Let me point out that I'm the type of person who believes we should always listen to what others have to say before making a final decision. After all, your idea may be much better than mine, in which case we'll use your idea. However, what I learned that day was that it wasn't about Gwen decorating our house. Instead, it was about Cara getting permission from Gwen before making a single decision. And over the next sixteen years, Gwen's control over Cara would only grow exponentially.

The movers were gone, and the large pieces of furniture were in place, which meant we could sleep in our own bed that night. We still had many boxes to unpack but, fortunately, we had the entire week off from work to put things away and finish decorating the house. And before we returned to work the following week, we had actually emptied every box and were able to pull both vehicles into the garage. Most importantly, I was able to show Cara that she was great at decorating the house on her own.

The year 2008 was turning out to be an amazing year for us. We got married, spent our honeymoon taking a cruise (okay, so we missed the first two days), moved into our new home, and got a new Corvette and BMW.

Because I've been a car guy since I was very young, I had previously owned other Corvettes, but this would be my first new one (another first in our lives together). Because Cara had never been married, she couldn't afford a BMW (which had been her dream car for years) on her own. So, even though it took a while to find the exact one she wanted, I finally found a white 328xi with a beige interior online early one morning.

The car was in Dallas, so I had to close the deal over the phone. I'll always remember how happy she was when I got off the phone and told her, "You better get ready, we have to drive to Dallas to pick up your new car."

"Are you serious?" she cautiously asked.

"Yes," I said, "it's a done deal."

She was so thrilled as she walked over to me and gave me a long hug. It was moments like those that I wish could have lasted forever. But I guess it's just not possible.

To finish out the year with a big bang, I surprised Cara by asking her, "2008 has been our year, what would you say to doing something spontaneous to close it out?"

"What are you thinking about doing?" she asked.

"Let's fly to Vegas for the New Year celebration," I suggested.

"Have you ever done that before?" she asked.

"No, I haven't. Have you?"

"No, I haven't either."

"So, it would be another first for us," I pointed out.

"Okay, let's do it." She smiled.

I immediately got online and started checking flights. I quickly learned that we had waited far too late to try to book a non-stop flight to Vegas in time to celebrate the New Year. After a few minutes, I gave up and called a travel agent for assistance. It turned out that they, too, couldn't find us a non-stop flight, but they were able to book us a layover flight to Vegas. The only drawback was that the first leg of the flight into Denver would be on an older, smaller turboprop plane.

We were so excited to be doing something so unplanned that we didn't care what type of plane we'd be flying on. That is, until we were approximately thirty thousand feet in the air. Then, it felt like all hell was breaking loose when we encountered the worst turbulence either of us had ever experienced.

Ironically, after boarding the plane, I reassured Cara that the older turboprop planes were very reliable. It was only after the plane was being tossed around the sky like a kite in a windstorm that I began to have doubts. I had to reassure myself more than once during the flight that the aircraft was genuinely as safe as I'd believed it to be. Fortunately, we eventually escaped the turbulence and landed safely in Denver.

It took us a while, but we did calm down enough to joke about it and enjoy the last leg of the flight to Vegas. And most importantly, we arrived in time to check into the hotel, drop our luggage off in the room, and make it back down to the street before midnight and the New Year celebration. It was a spectacular way to finish the year. For both of us, it seemed like our dreams were finally coming true.

If 2008 was our year, and what we believed to be the beginning of an amazing life together, it appeared that 2009 didn't get the memo. On February 10, 2009, an unusually early time of year for a weather event like this, a severe thunderstorm came through our area and destroyed the roof of our new home.

In all my years being a homeowner, I'd never lost a roof on a house. Now, when our house was only seven months old, the roof was severely damaged and would need to be replaced. But that wasn't what had my head spinning the most. It was the date of the thunderstorm and the fact that it was an extremely unusual weather phenomenon for that time of year. February 10, 2009, was exactly fourteen years after my first ever date with Lorrie. I tried convincing myself that it was just a coincidence, but I knew it wasn't. What I didn't know was whether it was karma, an omen for what was to come, or both.

One of the worst-kept secrets in Fresenius was that Regional Vice President Don had a girlfriend in Texas, while his wife still resided in Oklahoma. However, when Don was fired from the company, the reasons for his termination were kept quiet. As acute services manager, I was privy to this information, but I never disclosed it to anyone other than Cara. And while the rumor mill was blowing up, most of the rumors were incorrect and some even ridiculous. It was like so much of the information that you see online today—occasionally, there's some merit to a conspiracy theory, but usually they're just absurd.

Cara was very surprised to learn that Don was no longer working for the company. She had known him for many years and thought he was one of the untouchables. I was surprised, yet grateful, to see that she didn't really care one way or the other anymore. I actually thought she might still be angry with Don because he had prevented her from moving into the Education Department years earlier, but I was wrong. And I have to say that it was nice to know she was happy with the way her life was going and no longer held any ill will toward him.

Maybe there was some truth to that old saying, "Living well is the best revenge." And maybe I had something to do with her happiness at the time. Or maybe she was just happy because she knew her plan was in place, moving along at just the right tempo, and I was oblivious to what was really happening in my life.

As we settled into 2009, I was becoming burned out from overseeing one of the largest acute dialysis units in the country. At one time, I had fourteen contracts with various hospitals in Oklahoma City. That's a lot of nephrologists and hospital administrators to keep satisfied.

The money was great, especially when the bonus arrived each year, but I wanted to spend more time with Cara and less time working.

It was also during that time that Cara was thinking about making a change out of the Education Department. She wanted to move into Home Therapies. Fortunately for her, I was able to make a phone call to the unit's manager, Kristie, and let her know that Cara was thinking about making a change. Kristie told me they had an opening and that if Cara wanted the job, it was hers.

After getting off the phone, I explained to Cara that if she wanted the position, all she needed to do was call Kristie. In no time at all, Cara turned in her resignation and moved over to Home Therapies, where she would work until she retired.

Before I made a final decision to leave the Acute Dialysis Department, I received a call from Tammy, one of the area managers, asking if I had any openings in the acute unit. I explained that with the high burnout rate I was always looking for additional nurses, especially with acute dialysis experience. Tammy said that she was calling as a favor for a nurse but that she was not asking for any favors from me. I had known both Tammy and her husband, Jim, for several years, and because they had been so good to me I would have been happy to do a favor for her. I did, however, notice that Tammy appeared to be a little nervous and almost afraid to tell me the nurse's name. When she did finally say his name, I couldn't believe my ears.

"Tammy, did you just say Don?" I cautiously asked.

"Yes," she said, "but I'm not asking you to hire him."

"Is there a reason he didn't call me, himself?" I asked.

"He said he doesn't know you that well, so he asked me to call you for him," she explained.

"Okay."

"Kenny, I think he believed he might have a better chance getting hired if I called you."

"Tammy, I'm not sure if you know this, and I'm not at liberty to elaborate, but Don's a no-rehire."

"Oh, my God!" she exclaimed. "No, I didn't know that, Kenny, or I wouldn't have called you."

I could tell she was embarrassed hearing this, so I assured her it wasn't a problem at all.

"Tammy, you know I'd help you if I could, but I can't hire Don," I explained.

"I know, and I'm so sorry."

I told her she had nothing to be sorry about and that if it had been anyone other than Don, I probably could have helped her. She understood, and we ended the call.

Later that evening, I told Cara about my conversation with Tammy.

"Cara, do you realize what happened today?" I asked her.

"Yeah, Don asked Tammy to talk to you about a job in acutes," she calmly replied.

"No, sweetie, that's not what I mean. I want you to think about the big picture for a minute."

I paused for a moment to see if she'd reply, but she didn't. She just looked at me like she didn't understand what it was that I was asking of her.

"Honey, the guy who blacklisted you and prevented you from going to work in the Education Department, who was fired from the company, reached out and indirectly asked your husband for a job today." I paused to let it all sink in. "Other than maybe our roof being destroyed on February 10," I joked, "I don't think I've ever seen karma work like this before. And it's not like I'm being vindictive. He's a no-rehire, so I couldn't hire him even if I wanted to."

"I understand what you're saying," she said, still devoid of any emotion at all. "I guess I'm at a point in life that I just feel sorry for him."

"I'm glad you feel that way, but I guess I'm still trying to wrap my head around all of it," I said. "I think the universe is so much more powerful than any of us can imagine."

We didn't talk about it again the rest of the evening, but I couldn't help thinking about how everything had come full circle. The fact that we had nothing to do with any of it put the power of the universe on full display for me to see that day. It also scared the hell out of me when I thought about how much I had hurt Lorrie when I left her for Cara. Was what happened to Don a sign of things to come for me? Was the loss of the roof just the beginning of it? After all, Don appeared to be on top of the world when he was terminated. He had a home in Oklahoma, a nice apartment in Texas, access to the company jet (which he used on a regular basis), a nearly unlimited expense account, and a high-paying position that most of us could only dream of.

I wanted to believe that I was nothing like Don, but I had hurt someone who cared dearly for me. And now, after getting the call from Tammy, I was envisioning every scary scenario that I could imagine. But what I didn't realize at the time is that karma can come up with circumstances that most of us can't even conceive.

Jennifer

It was late 2009 when I decided to leave Fresenius and accepted a state position with the Oklahoma Health Care Authority. In doing so, I was able to transfer my sixteen years with the University of Oklahoma and my state retirement over to my new position. Therefore, when I was ready to retire, I would have a nice state retirement to augment my social security retirement.

After working as acute services manager for three and a half years, I could tell the stress of the job had taken a toll on me. I was hoping that by moving back into a state position, the endless long hours and overwhelming stress would come to an end, which they did.

When I accepted the offer for the state position, I began as a senior reviewer in the Prior Authorization Unit. It was a nice change of pace with wonderful hours, but it was also a lot less money. In fact, my pay was cut by $33,000 dollars per year to make the move. It was a tough pill to swallow, but I reminded myself of how much my quality of life had improved. And with Cara working in her new position, which was located only a couple of miles from where I worked, we could now commute to work together—something we couldn't do at Fresenius because of the long hours I worked.

The Prior Authorization Unit was co-managed by Cecelia and Maria. They divided their management duties, but they both had equal authority over all the employees in the unit. Fortunately, both of them were very kind, caring nurses who treated all of their employees with a great deal of respect. I truly enjoyed working for them, and it was a nice change of pace from dialysis nursing. And, like many state jobs, it came with set hours, and weekends and holidays off.

As I settled into my new position and began getting to know the staff, I also met Jennifer Trevino, who was close friends with Cecelia. Jennifer was a supervisor in the Care Management Unit, located near the Prior Authorization Unit.

As I got to know her, I learned that Jennifer was a reservist with the 507th Medical Squadron and chief of the immunizations clinic, and that she had earned the rank of captain. Jennifer was very friendly and openly spoke about her children and ex-spouse, and the problems she had experienced with a younger ex-boyfriend.

It sounded like her relationship with the father of her children was amazing. He was an attorney, and they seemed to get along well. However, the ex-boyfriend was a different story. At first, it didn't sound like anything that most of us hadn't experienced in our lifetime. But as time went on, their relationship became much more abusive, and Jennifer had begun to fear him.

Jennifer joked around like it was no big deal, but it was obvious that she was just putting up a good front. Cecelia later told me that when Jennifer broke up with the ex-boyfriend, he showed up unannounced at the Health Care Authority carrying flowers. Because the staff working the front desk recognized him, he was allowed to walk freely back to Jennifer's office. Cecelia said that Jennifer called for security and had him removed from the building. James, the head of security, then made it clear that no one, including employees, was allowed into the building unless they had their state-provided badge or were accompanied by an employee with a state-provided badge. Therefore, anyone without a badge would remain in the lobby and wait for an employee with a badge to come and get them. Then, all visitors would have to sign in and out when entering and exiting the building. This change was still in effect when I retired from the agency.

When I hadn't heard any more about the ex-boyfriend harassing Jennifer for quite some time, I figured that he had finally moved on, but I was wrong. Cecelia told me that when Jennifer went home one afternoon, she found that he had broken into her home but ran out the back door when she came in. This would be the event that convinced Jennifer to seek a protective order against him, which she was in the process of doing.

I told Cecelia that this guy was scary, and I was glad to hear that Jennifer was taking legal action against him. I also found out that she had previously taken legal action against him when he physically assaulted her. Sadly, he pleaded guilty to a misdemeanor assault and got a one-year suspended sentence. Although I knew that a protective order may not be worth the paper it was written on, I was hopeful that the threat of jail may get him to finally move on and leave Jennifer alone. Again, I was wrong.

In July 2010, Cara's family all got together for another family vacation in Pagosa Springs. This year, we weren't able to stay the week of July 4 and had to go a couple of weeks later. It meant that we wouldn't get to see the fireworks display put on by the local community for Independence Day, but there were many other things to see and do in the area, so it was still a great place to spend a week with family.

The time spent in Pagosa Springs went extremely well and it appeared that everyone was having a great time. Cara and I had driven to Durango twice that week to shop and have lunch together. The drive was only about an hour, and the scenery was so beautiful that it made it worthwhile.

Then, early one morning while we were making plans for the day, I received a call from Cecelia. I remember her voice was quivering when she told me that Jennifer had been murdered by her ex-boyfriend.

My first thought was that I couldn't believe what I had just heard her say. My next thought was that this was the second time a coworker I personally knew had been murdered. It was also the second time

Cara and I were on vacation in Pagosa Springs with her family when I received news about someone I knew being murdered. It just didn't seem realistic to me. I think I must have been in mild shock for the rest of the conversation as Cecelia filled me in on all the details she had at the time.

As it turned out, Jennifer's ex-boyfriend, Brandon Hulin, a very mentally disturbed young man, had kidnapped Jennifer from her home and forced her to go with him to Lake Hefner, where he had parked his car. The evidence showed that he assaulted Jennifer while in her car, and then the two of them ended up in his car, which he drove to a hotel in Norman, leaving her car parked at the lake. I'm not exactly sure when he shot Jennifer, but I do know that after murdering her, Brandon left her body in his car and then went into a room at the hotel. After a standoff with police, Brandon committed suicide in his hotel room.

Cara had been listening to my end of the call and was able to piece together what had taken place. When Cecelia and I concluded our conversation, I shared everything that I could remember with Cara. She was as shocked by the news as I was.

Cara and I both found it hard to believe that Jennifer had been murdered by her ex-boyfriend. First, Randy was murdered by his girlfriend's ex-boyfriend and now another coworker had been murdered. What in hell was happening?

I returned to work the following week, and the atmosphere was solemn. So many people knew Jennifer, but even for those who didn't know her, the fact that a coworker had been murdered was so difficult to comprehend. We see those stories on television shows like "Dateline," but most people never experience the loss of a coworker to a murder-suicide.

Because Jennifer was originally from Auburn, Indiana, her family had decided to return her body home to be laid to rest. However, because Jennifer also had so many friends in Oklahoma, the family held a service for her in Oklahoma City before taking her body back home to Auburn. So, one week after she was murdered, on Wednesday, July 21, 2010, many of us gathered at the People's Church to say one last goodbye to Jennifer, or Jenny to those of us fortunate enough to have had the pleasure of befriending her.

After the Honeymoon Phase

In retrospect, I refer to the first three years of our marriage as the best years of our lives together. Those three years were truly a honeymoon phase. It seemed as though everything had gone our way, and we were both very happy. What I didn't know was that just around the corner lurked an event that would change the trajectory of our lives forever and move us into the next stage of marriage. But before this event, Cara and I were still acting like kids and having fun. One of the childish things I loved to do was to hide somewhere in the house trying to scare Cara when she walked back into the room. I'm not sure why I found it so funny, but I did. Cara would always tell me that I was a little kid in a man's body, and I always gladly agreed with her. But one night, she decided to turn the tables on me. To this day, I still don't know how she pulled it off, but she did.

It was late, and we were getting ready for bed. I wanted a drink of cold water. Cara had just gotten in bed and the house was dark, so I cautiously walked from the bedroom into the kitchen. I was pretty comfortable with the layout of the house, so I didn't feel the need to turn on any of the lights.

I opened the refrigerator door, grabbed a water bottle and took a few sips. I then closed the refrigerator door, leaving me in the dark again. Having previously performed this ritual many times, I knew to allow enough time for my eyes to adjust to the darkness before returning to the bedroom. However, as I slowly turned around, I saw someone standing directly in front of me.

"Son of a bitch!" I screeched as I quickly backed up against the refrigerator.

It took me a few seconds to realize that it was Cara standing next to me. She had no expression on her face, just staring at me.

"How the hell did you get in here without me hearing you?" I asked her, nervously chuckling. But she didn't reply. She just stood there staring at me. I was beginning to get a little creeped out by her lack of emotion, but I knew she was just getting even with me for all the times that I had scared her.

"I'm ready to go to bed now," I slowly said as we smiled at each other.

Without saying a word, Cara turned around and began walking away. I followed her into the bedroom and watched her get back in bed. It was obvious that she had scared the hell out of me, but it's those child-like moments that I hope I'll remember forever. Because, sadly, the fun and games were about to come to an end.

I had begun experiencing sciatica again that wouldn't clear up, and it turned out that I would need a third back surgery to correct the problem. Having previously had two back surgeries and a tonsillectomy, I was no stranger to surgery, but this would be my first surgery since meeting Cara.

I asked her to come with me to meet the neurosurgeon and let me know what she thought about him. She agreed, and after another MRI, we met with the surgeon in his office.

He went over the MRI results and recommended a discectomy and fusion with the addition of artificial implants. I had previously been through a partial discectomy, so I understood that the recovery process could be pretty tough. However, my past back surgeries had gone well and I had made a full recovery after both, so the surgeon said that I should make a complete recovery after this procedure, too.

As we looked over the image results, displayed in the light box hanging on the wall, the surgeon pulled out a model of a spine with spinal fusion hardware. He explained this was the type of hardware he would be using on me. I asked why the hardware was required, and he explained that it would be used to hold the spine and implants in place until the fusion fully healed. The hardware would no longer be needed after the fusion healed, but removing it would require another major surgery, which was why it would be left in the body.

As the physician continued with his explanation, I began feeling overwhelmed. It wasn't the same as that little voice trying to tell you something, but it was still an uneasy feeling.

"I'm not going to have the surgery," I told Cara, the surgeon, and the physician's assistant.

"What's wrong?" Cara calmly asked me as the surgeon and his assistant sat quietly and listened.

"I feel like something's wrong, and I don't want that hardware left in my body," I explained.

The room fell silent and everyone was looking at me, waiting to see what I was going to say next, but I didn't say anything. I just sat there in silence.

After what seemed like an eternity, Cara reached over and held my hand. Gently squeezing it, she looked into my eyes and said, "It's going to be okay."

I immediately felt my body calm down, which is something that Cara had always been able to do to me since we began dating. Anytime I found myself getting worked up, she had a way of making me feel calmer just by touching me and speaking soothingly.

"Okay, I'll do it," I relented.

The physician proceeded to explain the procedure and the recovery process. I heard what he was saying, but my mind was still thinking about the hardware that was going to be left inside my body. I was also still trying to process the overwhelming feeling I had experienced when learning about the hardware. I hadn't encountered that feeling with either of the previous back surgeries, but this would be the first time that a foreign object would be left inside my body after a surgery.

Before leaving the physician's office, we scheduled the surgery for late January 2011. I was hoping that I would have enough time to recover before our third anniversary, which was on March 1, 2011.

Although I had always celebrated anniversaries in my previous marriages, they seemed so much more important with Cara. As I've previously stated, I believe it's because I had never been in love with anyone before her. So, for the first time in my life, I wanted to get it right and do something nice for her on every date that had a special meaning to us. For example, when I learned that Cara's mother would put a card and chocolate on Cara's bed every Valentine's Day when she was a little girl, I began doing the same thing every year. It seemed to bring her so much joy, which made me feel like I was finally learning how to be a good husband.

All of the necessary plans were in place, but as the surgery date approached, I began experiencing so much anxiety that it was really making me question my decision.

"Cara, I really feel like something is wrong and this surgery is not going to end well," I tried to explain.

"You mean like you're going to die?" she asked me.

"No, it's not that," I assured her. "I don't know what it is, but it's an overwhelming feeling that something is wrong."

She did her best to reassure me that everything would be okay. And I did my best to stop allowing the negative thoughts to cause me so much anxiety.

It was the week before the surgery when I started having flu-like symptoms. I tried to convince myself it was just allergies, or possibly a rhinovirus, the most common type of cold virus. But with every day growing nearer to the date of the surgery, I continued feeling worse.

I finally headed to an urgent care clinic for an examination, and the results were not what I wanted to hear. I learned that I had the flu, which explained why I was feeling so run down. I explained that I had an upcoming surgery and wanted to know if I would be well enough to undergo it. The young doctor explained that I would not be well enough to undergo surgery, leaving me no choice but to reschedule it. I couldn't believe what he had told me, but I was so sick that I didn't really care at that moment. I just wanted to start feeling better.

Years later, reflecting on that time, I now believe the universe was trying to tell me to listen to that little voice and cancel the surgery altogether. Sadly, I didn't heed the warning.

I called to reschedule the surgery, but the only date available was March 1, which was the date of our third anniversary. When I explained that I didn't want to have surgery on our anniversary, the surgical coordinator said she would need to speak with the physician's assistant to see how they wanted to proceed.

Later that day, when Cara came home from work, I brought her up to speed and told her I was waiting for the surgical coordinator to get back with me. Cara's response to the situation caught me off guard.

"If you put this off too long, the surgeon will probably want to see you in his office again before he'll do the surgery," she pointed out.

"I know you're probably right, but I do not want to have surgery on our anniversary," I tried to explain.

"It's your decision," she said, "but I think you should schedule the surgery and we'll celebrate our anniversary after you're feeling better."

"Okay. I'll call his office in the morning and see if the date is still available."

I really didn't want to have the surgery on our third anniversary, but the following day, I reluctantly called the surgeon's office and scheduled the surgery for the morning of March 1, 2011.

The feeling that something was wrong immediately returned, and it took everything I had to push that feeling aside. I didn't want to undergo a major surgery with so many negative thoughts going through my mind. However, I've since learned that when that little voice is screaming at you, it's best to listen to what it's trying to say.

On Tuesday, March 1, I had the surgery, and life as we knew it changed forever. I spent three days in the hospital before being released on Friday. I spent the next several weeks recovering at home. Cara stayed home with me the week following the surgery before returning to work, but then I was on my own during the day afterward. It was a rough few weeks, but I'm a typical Type A personality, and I pushed myself hard to recover as quickly as possible.

It would take several weeks to understand that I now had post-surgical neuropathy, which is caused by a nerve being damaged during surgery, as well as chronic back pain. Before the surgery, I had sciatica, which the surgery resolved. Unfortunately, while the sciatica was corrected, I now had new, more severe issues to deal with every day. I finally realized why I had been feeling so uneasy about the surgery and what that little voice had been trying to tell me. But it was too late to do anything about it.

I did my best to explain my symptoms to the surgeon, telling him that it felt like I had a severe sunburn from my waist down to the bottom of my feet, but on the inside of my body. The surgeon kept telling me that I needed to be patient and that it would eventually get better. But what he neglected to tell me was that the pain would never completely resolve itself and that I'd probably be on pain management for the rest of my life.

Although the surgery didn't go well for me, I didn't blame Cara at all for the outcome. At the time, I believed she was just doing her best to reassure me. Now, I believe it was important to Cara for me to have the surgery on the date of our third anniversary—all part of some bigger plan. I also blame myself for not listening to that little voice when it tried to warn me of what was to come.

Soulmates

I was approved to return to work about six weeks after the surgery, but I was still learning how to navigate through so much pain. My primary care physician at that time was attempting to manage my pain, and we began experimenting with various pain medications. I was prescribed gabapentin to help with the post-surgical neuropathy, which meant trying various dosages before we finally got the burning in my legs and feet mostly under control. I was willing to take large doses of the medication as long as it kept the burning at bay. Unfortunately, getting the chronic back pain under control wasn't meant to be.

It took several months of trying many different medications before finding a combination that allowed me to manage the pain enough to continue working. By that point, I had moved up from a senior position into a management position and was making much more money again. Unfortunately, this meant that I also had to deal with more stress, which would worsen the pain.

Although I give credit to my primary care physician for working with me, it was my relationship with Cara that helped me more than anything. She was there for me every step of the way and really understood how hard all this was on me. Some evenings after work, we wouldn't even turn on the television. Instead, we would sit together on the couch after dinner, hold hands and talk until it was time to go to bed. I loved those evenings so much because it felt like that time spent talking brought us so much closer together.

I had jokingly told her and others many times that she followed me into this world. But now it was no longer a joke to me. I sincerely believed it to be the truth. We acknowledged that we were soulmates, and I truly believed that the universe had sent her into my life for some reason. Cara also admitted on numerous occasions that she believed God had brought the two of us together. (In retrospect, maybe I should have asked her what God she was talking about.)

In all fairness, we also questioned why we had met when I was married, but I reasoned it away by saying that it was my fault. I explained to Cara that I should never have given in to Lorrie's ultimatum. Unfortunately, I've spent so much of my life trying to please other people that I often neglected to listen to that little voice when it was telling me to take care of my own needs. I further justified my decision to leave Lorrie by saying it may be part of a bigger plan that we didn't yet understand. Although I do believe there might be a bigger plan in place sometimes, I also acknowledge that this may just be something that we, as humans, tell ourselves to feel better about our decisions.

Cara acknowledged she understood my rationale for divorcing Lorrie but questioned her own decision for having an affair with me while I was married to Lorrie. I knew I didn't have the answer she was seeking, but I wanted her to understand that we're just as human and fallible as every other person on this planet.

"Cara, you've told me several times that you've judged one of your best friends for the decisions she made when the two of you were young, and how you would never do anything like that," I started. "But what if, sometimes, the universe shows us that under the right circumstances we're all capable of making decisions that hurt others?"

"Maybe you're right," she said. "I told myself I would never be with a married man. But I didn't know I was going to fall in love with you."

"Sweetie, I love you more than I've ever loved another human being," I told her. "And I'm not comparing our love to the love I have for my children or that we have for our parents. That's a different kind of love. I'm talking about the love you have for a partner."

"I know what you're saying," she assured me. "I've never loved anyone the way I love you. I just wish you hadn't been married to Lorrie when we met."

"I couldn't agree more. But I wish you wouldn't be so hard on yourself," I sympathized. "I could be wrong, but I don't think the universe would have put us together if it wasn't meant to be."

"I agree."

This was a conversation we had on more than one occasion, and I've often wondered if it was because we both carried so much guilt for hurting Lorrie. I can't speak for Cara, but I know that, after all these years, I still feel guilty for the pain I caused Lorrie.

At this point in our relationship, I had no doubt that Cara and I were soulmates with a deep cosmic connection. But it was still nice when the universe would surprise me and reaffirm my beliefs.

"Did you use to wear glasses at work?" Cara asked me one day.

I was dumbfounded by her question, which seemed to come from out of left field.

"I wore glasses for a short time before I switched to contacts," I replied.

"Were you wearing glasses when you worked for Bone and Joint?"

I was curious to see where she was going with her line of questioning.

"Yes, I had just started wearing glasses on a full-time basis when I went to work for them," I answered.

"Do you remember asking someone where the dialysis unit was located in the hallway at Saints?" Cara asked me.

I paused and just stared at her as I visualized that moment in time.

"Yes, I did ask someone for help," I cautiously answered.

Cara paused, looked into my eyes, and then softly said, "That was me."

The room was silent as we stared at each other.

"Oh, my God!" I exclaimed. "Are you serious, Cara?"

"Yes. I had just walked out of the dialysis room, and we were the only two people in the hallway," she reminded me.

"This is so bizarre!" I cried out. "I couldn't find anyone to ask for help and then out of nowhere, you appeared in the hallway." I attempted to keep my voice down. "I can't believe that was you!"

I don't know why it hadn't come up before, but this was almost too much for me to believe. The beautiful lady that I had encountered in the hallway of Saint Anthony Hospital so many years earlier was now my wife. Once again, the universe had just shown me how powerful it can be. I was going through one of the toughest times in my life, struggling with chronic pain and the side effects of the medication. But I had just learned that the lady, who I believed had been sent to me by the universe, had helped me all those years earlier.

"How long have you known that it was me in the hallway?" I asked her.

"I didn't know for sure until just now," she answered.

"Cara, you do know that it's no accident that we're together," I told her. "There's something very special about our relationship."

"I agree." she said before walking over and hugging me.

I already believed that Cara and I shared something special, but now I was convinced more than ever that our relationship was not some random accident. Whatever was happening was so much bigger than us. And the timing couldn't have been more perfect. The next few years would continue bringing us closer together as we dealt with tragedy and loss.

Maybe it was the tragedies, or the fact that I truly believed I had found my soulmate, that made me stop being so cautious and completely let down my guard. I'm not sure why, but I had finally reached a point where I trusted Cara more than any other soul on the planet. I shared this information with her, and she acknowledged that she had the same trust for me. So, it didn't surprise me that when we were getting ready for work one morning, she said, "You know, the only thing that we haven't done is combine our money."

"I know you're right, Cara, but I don't ever want to put myself in a position again where anyone can take everything from me," I explained.

"I understand," she said. "But I would never do that to you. And I'm not going anywhere. I will never give up on us, Kenny!"

I nodded in acknowledgment, and we continued getting ready for work. I believed every word she said, and I really did trust her, but that little voice was still trying to caution me. It wasn't screaming at me like it had in the past, but it was still making its presence known.

Maybe the universe was trying to remind me that when I met Cara, she owned a small two-bedroom home in an older, yet nice, neighborhood, but she didn't have a lot of equity in it. And the only retirement she had was a Primerica account that her brother-in-law had set up for her many years earlier. After we got married and I began handling our finances, I learned that not only had she not made any profit after investing in the account for nearly twenty years, but she had actually lost just over fourteen thousand dollars of her principal investment. When I discovered the loss, I had her pull all the money out of the account, and we wrote the losses off on our taxes over the next five years. I also helped her open up a matching 401k and managed the investment for her along with my investments.

I took a couple of weeks to think about it before telling Cara that I agreed with her about combining our finances. After all, if we were truly committed to each other forever, then we needed to do more than just talk about it. Shortly thereafter, we went to the bank and made the necessary changes to combine our finances.

Six Years of Hell

What I've come to learn about life is just how deceitful it can be. In my experience, life will throw you a bone to convince you that it's your turn and good things will soon be coming your way. Then, as you begin letting your guard down with cautious optimism, life hits you upside the head with a fastball.

It was 2013, and I was two years into a six-year period that I believed to be straight out of hell. Between the years of 2011 and 2017, Cara and I had to endure more tragedy than I thought was humanly possible. Well, actually, I had to endure the tragedies, but Cara was there with me.

It began with my third back surgery on March 1, 2011—our third anniversary—and paused on April 4, 2017. I wish I could say all of the tragedies came to an end that day, but I can't. Instead, it was as if the entity responsible for inflicting pain and suffering upon us just sat quietly for a few years before unleashing another reign of terror.

I had worked my way up to a director's position with the Oklahoma Health Care Authority. This was a high-ranking position, and I was earning more money than I had ever earned before. Financially speaking, it was one of the nicer things to come my way. However, the position also came with a lot of responsibility, which I took very seriously. But as I previously mentioned, I've learned that life can turn on you at any time.

I learned to cherish every good moment in life and keep moving forward like nothing bad will ever happen to me again. It may not be the right choice for everyone, but it worked for me. And it wasn't like

I was burying my head in the sand and hiding until all the evil in the world had passed. I learned that I have very little control over most of what happens in life, and I don't want to waste the good times waiting for the next bad thing to happen. If it's going to happen, it will happen, and all the worrying in the world won't change it.

Early Saturday morning, September 21, 2013, I received a call from my brother, Roger, explaining that our mom was on a ventilator in the hospital. Mom had suffered from pulmonary fibrosis for about six years but this was the first time she had been admitted to the hospital. Cara and I packed our suitcases and drove to Springfield, Missouri, as quickly as possible. My sister, Terri, was living in Italy at the time, so she didn't arrive until the following day. But at least all three of us kids had made it before anything worse happened.

By the end of the week, Mom was taken off the ventilator and moved out of the intensive care unit to a step-down unit for patients with respiratory issues. We did, however, understand that when she left the hospital she would be returning home on hospice, but she was stable for now. Hopeful that we had enough time to return home for a few days, Cara and I drove back to Oklahoma on Saturday, one week after arriving in Missouri.

I spoke with my dad frequently over the next couple of days, but on Monday afternoon, Terri called to tell me that mom wasn't doing well. I spoke with a nurse to ask if I had time to drive back to Missouri before it was too late, and I'll never forget when the nurse replied, "Probably not."

I felt terrible and didn't know what to do. I didn't want to be in Oklahoma waiting for that dreaded call to come, so I decided to drive back to Missouri and pray that I arrived before she died.

When I walked into Mom's hospital room around 9:30 p.m., I couldn't believe how well she was doing. Mom was sitting up in the bed, talking on the phone to someone. Dad was sitting next to the hospital bed, looking exhausted.

"What are you doing here?" Mom asked me.

"I came back to see you," I told her.

I immediately called Cara to let her know that I had arrived safely, and then I surprised her by putting Mom on the phone. She was as surprised as I was that Mom was doing so well. Mom was still short of breath, and because she had just been talking to someone else, she had to keep the conversation short. But at least she was able to speak to Cara for a moment. I told Cara that I'd call her in the morning with an update and said goodnight to her.

After an hour or so, Mom told Dad that he and I needed to go home and get some rest. I told her that I was going to stay at the hospital with her, but she insisted that I go with Dad. I was too tired to argue, so we said goodnight and Dad and I headed out.

As we walked down the hallway, we had almost passed the nurses' station when something strange happened to me. An intense feeling came over me that caused me to actually stop dead in my tracks. I remember Dad stopped and looked at me and asked, "Is something wrong?"

"I'm not sure, Dad. Do you think I should stay with Mom tonight?" I asked him.

"You can if you want, but she told you to go home and get some rest," he replied.

"Yeah, I guess you're right. I'm probably just tired from the drive," I said.

Dad and I got in our cars and drove to their house. Terri was already there, and I figured that she was probably staying in her former bedroom, where I always stayed when visiting Mom and Dad. My bedroom had been converted into an office for Mom shortly after I moved out in the late '70s. This meant that this time, I would need to sleep in Roger's former bedroom, which I had never stayed in until that night. It would also be the last night I would ever sleep in that bedroom.

This is when I'll mention that Mom and Dad's home is like a time capsule from the '70s. Nothing has been changed, including all the family photos that have been hanging on the wall since they were placed there when the house was still fairly new. For the three of us kids, it's like stepping back in time to a place where we felt so safe and secure. It's difficult for anyone else to believe that most everything is still original.

When I saw that Terri was staying in her former bedroom, I put my suitcase in Roger's old bedroom and started getting ready for bed. Terri was actually on the phone with Mom and, after hanging up, she said that Mom wanted to remind us to bring her hairbrush when we returned to the hospital in the morning. Dad placed the brush by his cell phone on the kitchen counter so we wouldn't forget it. We all said goodnight and went to bed. After sending out a couple of texts to coworkers, I turned off the light and went to sleep.

It was about 3:00 a.m. when I was awakened by the ringing of the house phone in Dad's bedroom, which was just across the hall from me. Considering the circumstances, I knew that any call coming in at that hour could only be bad news. I heard Dad's voice when he replied to the person on the other end of the line, but I couldn't tell what he was saying. And then his bedroom door opened and he knocked on the door to my room. I was already getting up, so I quickly opened the door.

"That was the nurse from the hospital. Your mother died," he said, his voice cracking as he fought back the tears.

I have never forgiven myself for not heeding the warning I received when Dad and I were leaving the hospital, nor do I think that I ever will.

The following year, 2014, I developed an abdominal hernia, which was most likely caused by the side effects of the medication I was taking on a daily basis. Fortunately, this would be one of the more insignificant issues that I had to deal with during this six-year time frame. And because I was able to have the hernia repaired via laparoscopic surgery on a Friday, I was able to return to work four days later, on Tuesday. This was my fifth surgery, but only my second surgery since Cara and I had been married.

Living in Oklahoma, I've seen more than my share of tornadoes, which is why I have a storm shelter in the garage of my home. I also have a very realistic understanding of that old saying, "The calm before the storm." This is the best way I can describe the year 2014 as compared to the following three years—2014 was the calm, and the years 2015, 2016, and 2017 were the storm.

It began in early 2015, when Dr. Kautilya Mehta, a well-known vascular surgeon, retired from surgery and came to work at the Oklahoma Health Care Authority. As a director, I had the opportunity to work closely with most of the physicians, including Dr. Mehta, and it wouldn't take me long to discover that he was a kind, caring soul. However, in all fairness, Dr. Mehta was also an old-school physician who believed nurses should stay in their lane. Therefore, it was difficult for him to understand how much authority some nurses actually possessed. I would experience this old-school behavior first hand when we attended our first off-site meeting together.

In late March of 2015, Senior Medical Director Dr. H. learned that he would not be available to attend one of our upcoming meetings with Telligen, so he asked Dr. Mehta if he would mind attending the meeting in his place. He explained to Dr. Mehta that, as a Health Care Authority representative over the Quality Assurance Unit, I would be in attendance and that I could answer any questions he might have regarding the meeting process. Dr. Mehta agreed, and he and I attended the off-site meeting together at Telligen's office.

A physician working with Telligen took the lead and directed the meeting, which was standard protocol. It was also standard practice for others, like myself, to ask questions regarding any quality assurance issues. However, throughout the meeting, I noticed that every time

I asked a question, Dr. Mehta would just glare at me. It was a little uncomfortable, but because this was my job, I wrote it off as Dr. Mehta's lack of experience with the Telligen meetings. I would later learn that it wasn't just his lack of experience with the meetings. It was the fact that he could only see me as a nurse and not as a director.

The following day, Friday, April 3, 2015, Dr. Mehta and I attended a briefing with Dr. L., who was the chief medical officer at the Health Care Authority, and to whom I directly reported. This was a routine briefing that took place after each meeting with Telligen to provide a status update to Dr. L.

Because I had previously attended dozens of these meetings with Telligen, I provided the update on that day. After the meeting concluded, Dr. Mehta attempted to make a joke to Dr. L. that he thought I was going to blow a gasket during the meeting with Telligen. I was clueless as to what he was talking about, but because it was his first time attending a meeting with Telligen, I tried to give him the benefit of the doubt. So, after he made the statement, I shrugged my shoulders to let Dr. L. know that I didn't understand what he was talking about. Dr. L. knew me well and knew that I always presented myself as a professional, especially when representing the Health Care Authority. Therefore, it was obvious that she didn't get it either, and she concluded the meeting.

During dinner that evening, I shared the story with Cara, and we had a good laugh about it. She knew Dr. Mehta from working with him years earlier at Saint Anthony Hospital. She had taken care of many of his patients in the intensive care unit, and she remembered he was one of those doctors who thought nurses should be seen and not heard.

It seemed odd to us that he could be so kind and caring to everyone and yet have such an old-school manner of thinking about the roles of doctors and nurses. Again, we laughed about it and even poked fun at him and some of the other old-school doctors who believed they could walk on water. After dinner, Cara and I went on to enjoy our weekend together before returning to work the following Monday.

There was nothing unusual about the morning, until an unscheduled meeting was announced. Dr. L. had requested a conference-room meeting with all her direct reports. As we all came in and began questioning each other, it was obvious that no one knew the reason for the meeting. Unfortunately, we wouldn't have to wait long to learn that Dr. Mehta had suffered a massive heart attack and passed away on Saturday, April 4, 2015. (April 4 would become a significant date in my life. I just didn't know it at the time.)

I couldn't believe what I had just heard or how much guilt I was experiencing. I rationally understood that I had absolutely nothing to do with Dr. Mehta's death, but I couldn't help but feel guilty upon hearing the news. I had just been making fun of him and his old-school way of thinking regarding nurses. Although I hadn't said anything mean about him, I still felt extremely guilty.

There would be one more death in 2015, and this time, it would hit very close to home.

Close friends of ours, Eddie and Katherine Cantrell, two of the kindest people I have ever known, enjoyed many of the same activities Cara and I enjoyed. I first met Katherine when she came to work at the Health Care Authority. She reported to another director but, because her office was next to mine, she frequently asked me questions about specific tasks she was performing.

I learned that Katherine and Cara had a lot in common, and I wanted to introduce the two of them to each other. Before long, Cara and I began spending time with Katherine and Eddie, and we all became good friends. At some point, after learning that Katherine had a twin brother who died from colon cancer at the age of forty-two, I agreed to become her surrogate big brother. Obviously, it was more of a joke between a group of friends, but I always treated her just like I treated my biological sister Terri. And, just as she loved spending time with my sister Terri, Cara also loved spending time with Katherine. Sadly, it wouldn't be much longer before Katherine needed a big brother to lean on.

I've learned that no matter how well we think we know someone, we don't always know what's going on in their mind. I thought I knew Eddie pretty well, but we all soon learned that he had secrets he didn't share with the rest of us.

According to Katherine, she and Eddie were arguing about something when he quietly got up, walked out the door, got in his vehicle and drove away. It was atypical for Eddie to leave during an argument, but Katherine said she thought he wouldn't be gone too long. However, when he didn't return home that night, she became very concerned and reached out to the police early the next morning. Unfortunately, she learned that there wasn't a lot the police could do, because Eddie was an adult and hadn't broken any laws.

Katherine was beside herself and didn't know which way to turn. Then, to make things worse, one of the police officers reached out to Katherine to ask if Eddie was suicidal. It turned out that the officer had run a check on Eddie's credit card to see if he was still in the area. He thought it might make Katherine feel better to know he hadn't left town. But instead, the officer learned that Eddie had purchased a shotgun and ammunition.

The next update we received about Eddie came from a police officer who informed Katherine that on June 17, 2015, Eddie took his own life with the shotgun he had just purchased. We were all devastated by this news, and I still struggle with not knowing how long Eddie may have suffered in silence.

It would be almost six months before we had to deal with another death in the family. This time it was Cara's father, Wayne Willis, who passed away from complications related to a chronic illness. Wayne died on December 6, 2015, at the age of eighty-nine. He was truly one of the best Christians and human beings I've ever had the pleasure of knowing. Wayne was a kind, gentle soul with a dry sense of humor who could always put a smile on my face.

By early 2016, it looked like things might be improving for us. Cara was still hurting from the loss of her father, but she still had her mother, and the two of them shared a special mother-daughter bond. And because Cara and I had experienced so much tragedy together, our relationship had only grown stronger, and we were closer than ever.

I honestly can't recall how many times a stranger would stop to tell us it was so obvious Cara and I were in love. We always thanked them and acknowledged that their kind words were true. It was always such an amazing feeling when this happened, and we would talk about it for days on end.

Things had slowly begun looking up for Katherine, too. Losing Eddie was such a devastating experience for her, but she had a lot of friends who all reached out to her in her time of need.

One friend who reached out to help her was one of my best friends, Brad. So, when Katherine told me that she and Brad had begun secretly dating, I had mixed feelings about the news. I couldn't have been happier for the two of them, but I was concerned that maybe Katherine was moving too quickly.

As I previously mentioned, I treated Katherine just like I treated my sister, Terri, and I would have had the same thoughts and feelings if Terri were going through a similar situation. Therefore, I was honest about my feelings when I spoke to both Brad and Katherine. I also mentioned that I had concerns about Brad's ex-girlfriend, who was the mother of his daughter. I explained to Katherine that I was concerned about her safety because of everything Brad had told me about his ex-girlfriend.

Katherine told me she understood and assured me that if it became too crazy, she would walk away. Then, after sharing my feelings with the two of them, I expressed how much I loved them and that I only wanted the very best for them and their relationship. That was the only time I ever mentioned my concerns to them.

Brad and Katherine's relationship jumped into high gear very quickly, and they both seemed so happy. So, when they told me that they were getting married and asked me to give Katherine away at the wedding, I was elated. I let them know how honored I felt to be part of their new life together.

On May 6, 2016, I walked Katherine down the aisle and waited to give her away to my good friend Brad. When the marriage officiant asked, "Who gives this bride away?"

I simply replied, "Standing in as her brother, I do."

Hearing those words, Katherine squeezed my hand and smiled at me. I then placed Katherine's right hand into Brad's left hand and returned to my seat. This would be one of the best moments I can recall happening that year.

The following month, I had a dorsal column stimulator implanted into my body. After months of researching outcomes, along with the assurance from a physician and physician's assistant that it was all but guaranteed to offer me some pain relief, I decided to trust them and give it a try. For those of you keeping count, this was my sixth surgery, but only my third surgery since getting married to Cara.

Late Saturday evening, July 9, 2016, only a few weeks after having the surgery, I received a phone call from my brother-in-law John. He and my sister lived in Lawton, Oklahoma, which is about eighty-five miles from our home. He wanted to let me know that Terri was back in the hospital and that she was stable, but she would probably not be released to go home for a few days. Because it was late, he suggested that we wait and drive down the following morning. I agreed with him, and we waited until the next morning to make the drive.

When Cara and I arrived at the hospital the following morning, we learned that Terri was in the intensive care unit. Feeling uneasy about the situation and like something was not adding up, we headed up to her room. The minute we saw her, we realized our concerns were warranted. Terri was unconscious and would never regain consciousness again.

On Sunday evening, July 10, 2016, my sister passed away from complications due to a long-standing chronic illness. She was fifty-five years old.

I was still recovering from the shock of losing my sister, as well as the most recent surgery, when more sad news hit me hard.

On Sunday, July 17, 2016, one week after Terri died, my uncle, George "Skip" Bass, and Brian Hughes, my best friend from high school, both died. Skip, who was living in Kansas at the time of his death, died from a chronic illness at age sixty-five. Brian, who was still living in Missouri where he had grown up, died from a heart attack at the age of fifty-seven. The two had only met on one occasion, when Brian and I were teenagers and drove up to Kansas for the weekend. Yet, they both died on the same day. It felt like I was in a nightmare and I couldn't wake up.

Because I had taken leave from work in June to have the dorsal column stimulator implanted in my body, I was nearing the end of my short-term disability benefits, which only lasted six months. I had met with the Medtronic representative on multiple occasions, but regardless of the settings that he tried, I never felt any relief from the pain. Now, after months of trial and error, I stopped charging the device and let it go dead. I was assured by the Medtronic representative that it was safe to leave it in my body and that no harm would come from it. That would soon prove to be incorrect. But at the time, I was facing a bigger issue.

I had continued working for nearly six years while taking large doses of pain medication. Unfortunately, every day was a struggle and it had taken a toll on my body. I loved my job, but it was a stressful position, which made managing the pain next to impossible. Cara and I had already made plans to retire in 2020, so retiring now would mean that I would be retiring approximately three and a half years early. I didn't know what to do, and I was running out of time.

After some lengthy discussions with Cara, we decided that I should meet with my primary care physician to get his input. He had been my family physician for over thirty years and knew my medical history better than anyone.

I scheduled an appointment, and I met with him the following week to discuss my dilemma. He wasted no time in telling me that regardless of how much I loved my job, it was time to retire. I followed his advice. In December 2016, I retired from my position as director of quality assurance and prior authorizations with the Oklahoma Health Care Authority.

Katherine

In March 2017, still reeling from how much devastation had occurred during the previous five years, Cara and I decided to take a break and go away for a while. We traveled to Hawaii for what we hoped would be a quiet, relaxing vacation. We had vacationed on the island of Oahu several years earlier and told ourselves that we wanted to return one day. But because of life's unexpected tragedies, we hadn't been able to return to the islands until now. So, on Monday, April 3, Cara and I flew to Oahu for some much-needed downtime.

We arrived in Oahu later that afternoon, took the shuttle bus to the resort, and checked into the hotel. Cara and I were both tired from the long flight, but I was wiped out from the chronic pain. Over the years, I've learned that if I can keep moving, or at least stand, it's easier to manage the pain. Unfortunately, I couldn't do either of those things during the eight-hour flight.

As soon as we were semi-settled into our room, we went back down to grab something to eat and then returned to our room. We had a beautiful view of the resort, beach and ocean, so we decided to sit on the balcony, relax and eat dinner while enjoying the view. It was the perfect end to a long day of traveling.

By early evening, we were both ready to call it a night and get some sleep. We wanted to feel rested before starting our vacation the following morning. We had already selected a few things we wanted to do, but we also told ourselves that we weren't going to pack in as many activities as we had done on our first visit to the island.

During our first trip, thinking we might not have the opportunity to make it again, we did as much as we possibly could. It was only after we returned home that we realized we had spent very little time relaxing. So, in hopes of not making the same mistake on this trip, we were going to limit our excursions.

After a good night's sleep, we got up and started our day. Because we're both planners, the first thing we did was stop by one of the concierge booths and book our main excursions for the week. We spent the next few hours walking around before stopping at a restaurant for lunch. Afterwards, we returned to the hotel to relax for a while before heading back out for the evening. It was just before noon when I took a few pictures from our hotel room balcony and texted Katherine.

Although Brad and I and Cara and Katherine were all close friends, Katherine and I were closer because of our sibling-like relationship. I think it was because she only had one twin brother, who had passed away about twelve years earlier, and I had always treated her like my biological sister. And now that Terri, my only biological sister, was gone from this planet, I think Katherine and I helped each other fill a void that was left behind with our siblings' passing. Regardless of how we got there, our relationship was never anything more than a loving, caring, big brother-little sister relationship, which Cara and Brad understood and respected.

Because Hawaii does not follow Daylight Saving Time, there was a five-hour time difference between Hawaii and Oklahoma from March 12, 2017, through November 5, 2017. So, when I sent Katherine three photos at 11:51 a.m., Hawaii-Aleutian Standard Time, it was 4:51 p.m. in Oklahoma. I sent her a text along with the photos.

"Cara and I decided to take one last big vacation, so here we are in Hawaii. This is the view from our room. We have two balconies and we're on the 18th floor. Sadly, traveling all day yesterday has taken a toll on me and I don't think I'll be able to travel this far again. Hope Brad is still feeling better. Take care, my friend."

A few minutes later, Katherine texted me back.

"Oh my goodness it's so beautiful! Thank you for sharing. That's probably as close as I'll ever get. Brad has had 3 good days which is awesome. It has actually seemed strange to see him walking normally, talking and smiling. It's been so long. I hope that you recover from the travel quickly and enjoy a wonderful vacation together!"

"Thank you, Katherine," I texted back. "I'm so grateful to hear Brad is feeling better. I'm going to increase the Rx to help the recovery process. I want to enjoy our time here. Take care."

Shortly thereafter, Cara and I headed out. We spent the afternoon milling around the shops at the resort before returning to our hotel room. Our first island excursion was planned for the next day, and we wanted to be rested up for the trip.

I don't recall what time we went to bed that night, but I remember Cara falling asleep, while I stayed up watching television. Then, around 11:30 p.m., I turned off the television and went to sleep.

It was just before 1:00 a.m. in Hawaii (and I had only been sleeping for about an hour and a half) when my phone rang. It was Vickie, a good friend of ours and Katherine's best friend. Laughing about the time of the call, I told Cara, "It's Vickie. I didn't tell her that we were going to be in Hawaii this week." Still laughing, I continued, "I'll let her leave a message and then call her later and explain what's going on."

Vickie had left a message, and I went ahead and listened to it. Thinking it wouldn't be anything too urgent, I was horribly shocked by Vickie's message.

This was the voice message Vickie left for me.

"Hi, Kenny, it's Vickie. Sorry to call so early in the morning, but Brad just got through calling me and said that Kat passed away. That's all I know about right now. I was just wondering if you heard anything different. If you did, give me a call. 405.xxx.xxxx. Thank you. Bye-Bye."

Having also heard the message, Cara sat up in bed.

"Did she just say that Katherine died?" she asked.

I faltered. "I'm not sure, but I think that's what she said," I replied in a panicked voice as I immediately began replaying the message. I wasn't sure that I had actually heard what I thought I'd heard, but Cara had heard it, too.

As the message played for the second time, we listened very intently and confirmed that Vickie had, in fact, said that Katherine had died.

Cara and I just looked at each other in disbelief.

"I wonder what happened?" Cara asked, dumbfounded.

"I don't know," I said, fighting back the tears. "I just texted with her a few hours ago and everything seemed fine."

"Maybe she had a heart attack."

"I don't know, but I'm going to call Vickie back right now."

I called Vickie, and when she answered, I could hear that she was crying. I put the phone on speaker so Cara could participate in the conversation. I explained that I hadn't heard from anyone but I was going to call Brad to find out what happened. Vickie then explained to us that Josh, Brad's seventeen-year-old son, had murdered Katherine.

My mind couldn't believe what I was hearing and my anxiety level was rising off the chart. I was numb with disbelief. I had known Josh for years and I never would have thought he was capable of harming anyone. He seemed like a very normal kid, who loved playing football and baseball.

After the call with Vickie, I called Brad and we talked for quite a while. My heart was breaking for him as he did his best to explain what had happened. What I remember most about the call is that he kept repeating, "I don't get it, Kenny. I just don't get it."

I did my best to try and comfort him, but this was new territory for all of us and I didn't know what to say. I just kept repeating, "I'm so sorry, Brad."

Brad explained that he, Katherine, and Josh had been arguing about Josh skipping school that day. He said it wasn't anything out of the ordinary, so he left to pick up his daughter from dance class.

However, when he returned, he noticed that Josh was acting a little strange, and he couldn't find Katherine. Then, while Brad was walking around the house looking for Katherine, Josh took his car and left. Brad said he finally walked into the garage, and that was when he found Katherine lying on the floor with a pillow over her head. In disbelief, he raised the pillow to find that she had suffered severe head trauma, at which point he called 911. He said the police and emergency services arrived at the house and within a very short time, Katherine was pronounced dead. All the details of how she was murdered would soon emerge.

After Brad left the house, Josh got a baseball bat and hit Katherine on the head, knocking her unconscious. In a panic, he dragged her body to the garage and left her lying on the floor. He later told authorities that after moving her body to the garage, he went back inside the house and sat quietly for about ten or fifteen minutes, thinking about what he should do next. Josh would also later say that he heard Katherine making a moaning sound, so he got a rifle from the closet, returned to the garage, and shot her in the head, ending her life.

So he wouldn't have to look at what he had done to her, he placed a pillow over her head and went back inside the house to wait for his dad to return home. Once Brad returned home, Josh took his dad's car and fled the scene. He was later arrested driving the stolen car near the Oklahoma-Kansas state line. He would eventually plead guilty to murder and be sentenced to forty years in prison.

I asked Brad to let me know once a date had been selected for Katherine's funeral service, so Cara and I could change our return flight home. Brad asked me when we were supposed to return home and I told him that it wasn't until the following Monday, April 10, 2017. He asked me not to change the date of our return flight and said he would try to have Katherine's funeral service on Tuesday, April 11. I agreed, and Cara and I stayed in Hawaii until the following Monday.

The remainder of our trip was a very somber time for us. We went through the motions, but it was very difficult to do anything without thinking about Katherine, Brad, Josh, and Vickie.

It was also difficult to understand why another coworker and friend had been murdered. This was my third coworker to be murdered, but this time it wasn't just another coworker, it was a very dear friend who was truly like my little sister. And once again, it happened while Cara and I were on vacation. None of it made any sense to me then, nor does it make any sense to me today.

These days when I think about Katherine, which is still fairly often, I try to remind myself of how fortunate I was to have had her in my life. I'm also grateful I texted her when I did and that she took the time to reply to me. However, I will admit that I still struggle with the fact that she was murdered only a few hours after we texted each other.

Misdiagnosis

Shortly after Katherine's murder, I began experiencing discomfort in my neck and weakness in my left arm. Concerned because of the issues I had experienced in my lower back, I made an appointment with an orthopedic surgeon. However, upon arriving at the clinic, I was told the surgeon was not in the office and that my only choices were to reschedule or to be seen by his physician's assistant. I was very familiar with the role of the physician's assistant, so I had no objection to keeping my appointment. Unfortunately, by the time I left the clinic that morning, I was terrified.

The physician's assistant had convinced me that I required neck surgery as soon as possible due to a high risk of paralysis. She made this determination based on the jerking movement in my fingers when she performed a neurological examination. I was so concerned when I left the office that I was scared to even step off a curb too hard, thinking that would be the end of my ability to walk.

On the way home from the appointment, Cara advised me that I should get a second opinion, and I agreed. Fortunately, one of her coworkers had worked with a neurosurgeon she trusted and highly recommended. Because my primary care physician had retired, I got a referral from my new primary care physician, Dr. K., and within a few weeks, I met with the neurosurgeon, Dr. N. I explained that I was concerned about the risk of paralysis, based on the information I received during my last examination. Dr. N. performed his own neurological examination on me and immediately put my mind at ease by explaining that I was no more at risk of paralysis than he was. He said that he would not recommend me having neck surgery at this point. I was relieved, and after weeks of stressing over misinformation, I could now relax and focus on what was causing my current neck and arm issues.

Dr. N. speculated that the dorsal column stimulator, which was still dormant in my body, may be contributing to the problem. He recommended having it removed. By this point, I believed Dr. N. to be an honest surgeon, so I scheduled an appointment and had every piece of the dorsal column stimulator removed from my body. Within a few weeks of having surgery number seven, the neck pain and weakness in my left arm were completely gone.

Because the surgery had gone so well, I asked Dr. N. about the titanium hardware that was implanted in my body in 2011. I explained that every winter, I'd been experiencing a freezing sensation in my feet (which was different from the pain caused by the post-surgical nephropathy), and that I would have to heat my lower back to ease the pain.

My theory was that the metal in my body was contracting due to the cold and that by warming up my lower back, the metal expanded, relieving the freezing sensation in my feet. Dr. N. explained that many patients with metal implants are impacted by temperature changes, but that he wasn't sure if removing the hardware would help. He did, however, say that based on how well I had done with the removal of the dorsal column stimulator, it was possible that removing the metal implant could relieve some of the pain.

That was all I needed to hear to agree to schedule surgery number eight. (I'm not sure why, but I still have the titanium hardware that was removed from my body during the surgery. Dr. N. had it sterilized and sealed in a clear container for me.)

After recovering from the surgery, the outcome was unbelievable. I could immediately feel a difference and the freezing sensation I had in my feet every winter was virtually gone. I had now undergone eight surgeries (five surgeries since Cara and I got married), but I was hopeful that this one would be my last.

A couple of years went by that were fairly unremarkable. That is, until 2020 arrived. But I don't need to tell you what happened that year. Most every living soul old enough to understand COVID-19 remembers what happened during 2020. My and Cara's lives were no more interrupted than anyone else's at that time, and like everyone else, we did our best to deal with it.

Although 2020 was definitely the year of change, not all the changes were bad, at least not for us. In August of 2020, Cara retired after thirty-three years of nursing. Now, we had more time to share with each other, which we had always loved doing and had done so well. I know spending too much time together can be difficult for some relationships, but we didn't feel that way. In fact, we had frequently talked about how we couldn't wait to be able to spend more time together.

I don't think I can explain in words how much I loved Cara or how safe and secure I felt when I was with her. I shared these feelings with her on a regular basis, and Cara always told me she felt the same way about me and how much she enjoyed spending time together. Truth be told, if I hadn't experienced it for myself, I'm not sure I would have believed in real-life relationships like ours. Before I met Cara, relationships like ours only existed in my mind and in heart-warming movies.

Cara and I had an eight-foot Christmas tree we put up each year. It had small, soft-white lights that created a calmness throughout the house. For Cara, it was about celebrating the birth of Christ, and for me, it was about the peacefulness of the holiday season. Thus, in keeping with tradition, the day after Thanksgiving, 2020, we continued with our annual ritual and put up the Christmas tree. Then, the two of us spent the holidays at home that year.

On January 1, 2021, we were taking the tree down to pack it away for another year when I noticed I was experiencing some mild shortness of breath. Cara asked me if I needed to go to the emergency room and get checked out, but I didn't think it was serious enough to warrant a trip to the hospital, so (although I had to stop and take frequent breaks) we continued putting away the Christmas tree and the decorations. I wasn't sure what was causing the shortness of breath, but I was hoping I would be better by morning. But I guess the powers that be decided it had been long enough since I last suffered.

By the next morning, I could tell that I was getting worse, but I still didn't want to go to the hospital. However, by that afternoon, I had changed my mind. Cara drove me to the emergency room, where I was diagnosed with bilateral pneumonia in my lower lobes. I did, however, test negative for COVID, which I think was a surprise for all of us. The emergency room doctor put me on an antibiotic and told me to follow up with my primary care physician.

A few days later, I followed up with my primary care physician, Dr. K., and once again, I tested negative for COVID. Unfortunately, whatever had caused this continued to cause me problems for the next few months. I would start feeling better and my lung capacity would improve, but then the shortness of breath would return. It wasn't making sense, and the symptoms wouldn't clear up and stay cleared up.

Because the condition had dragged on for a few months, my doctor decided to send me for another CT scan. This time, the scan would reveal much more than the previous scan I had in January. And the results were not good.

After receiving an email about my new lab results, I logged in to my account and read the report from the radiologist. I read it more than once to make sure that I hadn't misread the findings.

On May 7, 2021, I learned that I had pulmonary fibrosis and nonspecific interstitial pneumonia (NSIP). I was very familiar with pulmonary fibrosis, because this is the disease that claimed my mother's life. However, I wasn't familiar with NSIP, so I researched the diagnosis online before I said anything to Cara.

Cara was reading on the couch when I came into the living room and sat down on the loveseat across from her. She looked up at me and waited to see if I was going to say anything.

"I have some bad news I need to tell you," I said.

"What is it?" she asked.

"I just read the results from the CT scan," I explained, "and it's not good. It turns out that I have pulmonary fibrosis and NSIP."

"No!" she exclaimed. "Are you being serious?"

"Yes, I'm being very serious, Cara," I calmly replied.

I told her I still had the results pulled up on the desktop in the office, if she wanted to read it for herself. She got up and walked over to take my hand. Holding hands, we walked into the office together and sat down to read the report. Because neither of us was familiar with NSIP, I opened a tab with a detailed explanation and gave Cara time to read it. I had already read all of it, including the fact that it's terminal and there's not currently a treatment for the disease.

After reading through everything, we went back to the living room, sat down and began talking about it. I asked her to please not say anything to anyone until I had a chance to process all of it myself. (In retrospect, I'm guessing her first text was to her sister, Gwen.)

We were still discussing the new diagnosis when I received a call from Dr. K., who had just read the report and wanted to discuss the results with me. He was so kind and encouraging, telling me that he was going to make a referral to a pulmonologist, so I needed to hang in there and see what they said about it. I assured him that I would be okay and thanked him for reaching out to me. A few days later, I received a call from the office of Dr. P., and an appointment was scheduled for June 16, 2021.

Cara and I had a lot of late-night talks about the diagnosis and how I wanted to do things on my terms. We had previously set up our wills, living wills, and trusts, so I wasn't concerned about any of those items. However, I was concerned about the quality of life I would have, and I didn't want to reach a point where I couldn't take care of myself. Cara understood and said that she would support whatever decision I made.

On the morning of June 16, 2021, Cara and I drove into Oklahoma City to meet with Dr. P. After another chest x-ray and a pulmonary function test, we were taken into a room where we met with Dr. P. and his nurse practitioner, Samantha. Dr. P. didn't waste any time before giving me the good news. He explained that although I do have some mild pulmonary fibrosis (scar tissue) and nonspecific interstitial pneumonitis (inflammation) in my lungs, I do not have a terminal disease. He further shared that he saw this on a fairly regular basis, which can be rather scary for the patient.

The room went quiet as Cara and I looked at each other in disbelief. I had just spent forty days believing I had a terminal illness, only to find out that it was a misdiagnosis. It felt like I had been given a second chance at life.

Dr. P. suggested that I come back in six months, and if there were no changes (which he didn't expect to see), I wouldn't need any further appointments.

I followed up with Dr. P. on December 21, 2021, and everything looked great. Then, approximately one year after the initial diagnosis, my primary care physician ordered a follow-up CT scan, which showed no changes from the previous CT scan. And, in time, my shortness of breath improved significantly.

A Second Chance

Over the past few years, prior to being misdiagnosed with a terminal illness, I had slowly begun playing my bass guitar again in an attempt to get my chops back up to a level that would allow me to jam with other musicians. Because of my health issues, I had no intentions of playing the club scene again, but I was hopeful that I would meet other musicians with similar backgrounds with whom I could occasionally jam. Then, one morning while getting coffee, I met a guy who invited me to join him and a small group of friends that met for coffee one morning each week. It sounded like a great way to get myself out of the house and meet new people, so I accepted his offer and joined them for coffee the following week.

Over the next several weeks, I learned that two of the guys, Larry and Darrell (yes, their actual names), were musicians who played once a month for a prison ministry program, which was organized by The Bridge Church in Mustang, Oklahoma.

The men's program included members from the church who would pick up several non-violent prisoners and drive them back to the church for breakfast and worship service. During the singing and praise part of the service, Larry and Darrell would provide the live music. Both of the guys played guitar and sang, but they didn't always have a drummer or a bassist, which worked out well for me. I only played with them a few times, but I had no idea how big of an impact The Bridge Church would one day have on my life.

Shortly after learning that I was not terminally ill, and feeling like I had been given a second chance in life, I decided to make every moment count. So, once again, I pulled out my bass guitar and began practicing. Although I may not have been fully up to speed, I began looking for other musicians in the area who wanted to jam. Fortunately, it didn't take long before I met Jason and Stan, who rehearsed at Stan's house in Mustang (just south of Yukon).

The two of them had recently lost their bass player, and they played the same kind of blues and classic rock music that I was playing. So, after selecting a few songs, I joined them on Saturday for our first rehearsal.

It only took me one rehearsal to know that this was what I was seeking, and luckily, I was the guy they needed to complete a three-piece blues band.

Once again, it felt like things were falling into place for me. I still had to deal with chronic pain and the side effects of the pain medication, but things were improving. Anyone who has dealt with chronic pain understands the importance of your mental state when it comes to managing it. Therefore, spending time practicing and rehearsing with a band helped me so much psychologically that it also helped me physically.

We had only been rehearsing together for a few weeks when Stan shared some interesting news with me. After rehearsal one afternoon, he told me that although he didn't feel ill, he didn't feel a hundred percent, and he had also recently dropped about thirty pounds without trying to do so. The minute he told me that, the nurse in me kicked in and I started to worry about him. I didn't want to scare him, so I said, calmly, "Because you're a former smoker, I really think you should make an appointment and discuss this with your doctor."

"Yeah, I was thinking I probably need to make an appointment, but I've been putting it off," he replied.

"Hopefully, it's nothing, but I think it's better to be safe than sorry."

He assured me that he would make an appointment and keep us posted. I really wanted to believe that it was something other than cancer, but the symptoms that he described, along with his many years of smoking, had me very concerned.

After returning home from rehearsal and putting my equipment away, I shared with Cara what Stan had told me. She, too, was immediately concerned that something serious was going on in his body.

During rehearsals over the next few weeks, Stan told us he had made an appointment with his primary care physician, who made a referral to an oncologist. However, before Stan could go see the oncologist, he and his wife, Renee, both contracted COVID and he had to reschedule his appointment. I had only met Renee a few times, but she really cared for Stan and assured me that she would get his appointment rescheduled. But with Christmas and the New Year approaching, I wasn't sure how quickly she would be able to do so.

It was January 2022 when the band got back together to rehearse, and it was obvious that Stan's health was declining. He was now feeling weak and short of breath at times. And although he hadn't received a diagnosis from the oncologist, he was clearly very ill and quickly getting worse. Sadly, we would only be able to rehearse a couple more times before Stan was too weak to continue playing the drums.

I had recently introduced Cara to Stan and Renee, and she and I began bringing food to their house and helping however we could. I believe that Stan and I grew much closer after he became ill than we were in the previous months of playing music together. I think it's times like these that we realize what is truly important in life. And because Stan and I shared similar spiritual beliefs yet were both married to Christians, that also created a bond between us.

It was February 7, 2022, when a pulmonologist officially diagnosed Stan with cancer. Then, on February 9, 2022, an oncologist told Stan that he had squamous cell cancer and that it was inoperable. Stan's health was deteriorating very rapidly by that point, and he would be admitted to the hospital a couple of times before being released to go home one last time. On March 26, 2022, while sitting in his recliner in the living room, Stan passed away.

I didn't know it at the time, but Renee was a member of The Bridge Church in Mustang, where I had participated in the prison ministry program a few years earlier and where Stan's funeral service was to be held. Because the prison ministry program was held in another building on the church property, I had never been inside the main building until the day of Stan's funeral. If only I had been able to put the pieces together sooner, maybe life would have turned out much differently. But then again, maybe it wouldn't have made a difference at all.

One Last Goodbye

It had only been a couple of months since Stan passed away when Cara and I received a call regarding Cara's mother, Dean Ellen Willis, also called Deena by the grand-kids. Because I'm a big believer in cosmic relationships, I always found it interesting that Katherine's middle name was Deena, but Cara saw it as nothing more than a coincidence. Maybe she was right, and I was seeing a relationship that didn't really exist. I've had to accept the fact that there are many mysteries in the universe that we may never know the answers to.

Cara's sister Gwen reached out to let Cara know that she had received a call from a nurse at the assisted living center where their mother resided. The nurse informed Gwen that her mother had fallen and was lying on the floor in a great deal of pain. The nursing staff couldn't help her up due to the pain, but emergency services had been called, and the nursing staff were doing their best to keep her comfortable.

Cara and I immediately headed to the hospital, but because of a delay with the ambulance services, we didn't know how long it would be before her mother would be arriving. Fortunately, the local fire department had responded to the call and would be staying with Dean until the ambulance arrived. The paramedic on staff was able to administer pain medication, which helped manage her pain.

On our way to the hospital, we learned that the estimated arrival time would be a while longer, so we decided to reroute from the hospital to the assisted living center. This allowed Cara to be with her mother instead of waiting at the hospital for her to arrive.

Although it took longer than usual, the ambulance eventually arrived and transported Dean to the hospital for evaluation and treatment. Unfortunately, just as Cara and I had feared, the news was not good. Cara's ninety-two-year-old mother had broken her hip when she fell in her room. And now, her daughters would face one of the most difficult decisions of their lives.

The three sisters had to decide whether to allow surgery to be performed, with no guarantee that Dean would survive the surgery, or administer pain medication and keep her comfortable until she passed away. Cara had already discussed her decision with me, so I knew she did not want to put her mother through a major surgery and recovery that she probably wouldn't survive. However, she had to make sure that her sisters agreed.

After the surgeon answered all their questions, Cara and her sisters agreed that putting their mother through a major surgery would be exceptionally cruel, especially because she had stated numerous times that she was ready to reunite with her late husband Wayne, who she believed was waiting in heaven for her. So, after the decision was made to keep her comfortable, the physician requested that hospice be called to manage Dean's pain. It would only be a couple of days before Dean's suffering would come to an end.

By the end of Dean's first day in the hospital, most of the family members had gone home for the evening leaving Steve, Gwen, Cara, and me with Dean, who was sleeping comfortably. Although I can't remember how the conversation began, I do remember the four of us talking about dying, heaven, and family members that had passed away. To this day, I'm not sure why I decided to mention that I'm a spiritual agnostic and not a Christian, but I did. The moment the words came out of my mouth, Cara, Gwen, and Steve turned and stared at me. It was in that moment I realized I had just signed my own death warrant with Cara's family. If only I had kept my secret from Cara's sister Gwen, maybe I wouldn't be writing this manuscript.

On June 11, 2022, with her three daughters at her bedside, Dean opened her eyes as if she was looking at her daughters. And as they were telling their mother goodbye one last time, Dean took her final breath.

After Dean's passing, Cara and her sisters compared their mother's final moments to their grandmother's passing. She, also, opened her eyes just before she died.

I was standing next to Cara when her mother died, so when Dean opened her eyes, it did look as if she was looking at her daughters one last time. Sadly, this was probably not the case. Although I didn't say anything to them, this is actually a common occurrence in dying people due to the lack of muscle tone remaining in their bodies.

Two Tragedies, Part II

Because of the special bond Cara shared with her mother, I knew that Dean's passing would be extremely difficult for Cara, but I had no idea of the toll it would eventually take on her.

In the weeks following her mother's death, Cara had begun slipping into a deep depression. She was sleeping twelve to fourteen hours a night, napping several hours a day, and even reached a point where she didn't want to leave the house. Cara's reaction to her mother's death was very different than when her father passed away. Cara was close to her dad, but not in the same way she had connected with her mother. Maybe it was because Cara was the youngest of the three girls and lived at home with her parents during her years in nursing school. Whatever the reasons, there was definitely an undeniable bond between Cara and her mother that was much different than Dean's relationship to her two older daughters. And now that Dean was gone, Cara's struggle to cope with the loss of her mother was impacting both of our lives.

I did what I could to help her overcome her depression, but other than loving her and reassuring her that I was there for her, I was ill-equipped to do much else. At some point, I recommended that she speak with our primary care physician regarding her depression. She agreed, and after our physician modified her daily medication, she said she felt a little better. Unfortunately, it didn't do much to ease the pain of missing her mother.

In the past, before COVID changed the world, Cara and I had taken a nice, rejuvenating vacation almost every year since getting married. Although we had experienced terrible losses on two of our trips, when we learned about the murders of Jennifer and Katherine, our other getaways had been very enjoyable. Therefore, I suggested that we plan a nice vacation someplace we'd never gone before. Cara liked the idea, and we began planning a trip to Niagara Falls.

After researching the area, we decided to travel to Canada and explore some of the surrounding communities. Unfortunately, when we reached out to our travel agent, he said that everything was booked through late fall for the location we had selected. Because winters in that region could be very unpredictable, he recommended booking for the following year.

Frustrated, we decided to take another trip to Las Vegas instead. We had vacationed in the area a few times and knew we could always find plenty of things to keep us busy. So, in November 2022, we traveled to Las Vegas for a week. Just as we expected, there was a lot to do, and we had a great time. It may not have been a romantic getaway to Niagara Falls, but it was nice to get away from the stress of everyday life and spend some quality time together.

When we returned home, it seemed like things were back on track, and Cara began to heal and move forward after the loss of her mother. But as I have previously mentioned, it appears that every time life starts heading in the right direction, the powers that be become unhappy and need to upset our lives. But this time, life would hit harder than ever before, and once again, our problems would stem from interference from Cara's sister Gwen.

Gwen was the self-appointed matriarch of the Willis family, and she wore the title like a badge of honor. When I asked Cara why Gwen proudly took on this role, Cara would always downplay it and remind me that Gwen and Steve needed to control everything. I explained to Cara that I didn't mind them being in control as long as they stayed in their lane and left the rest of us alone.

I could talk to Cara about anything in the world except for her sister Gwen. Although I've tried, I've never understood the relationship between Cara and Gwen or the power that Gwen has over Cara. It was a mystery to me, and it often frustrated me when Gwen's control interfered with our plans. I tried to accept that this was just the way it was, and in all fairness, it was usually not anything too significant. So, it was difficult for me to understand when Gwen crossed the line and interfered in our finances. I never thought she would make a decision that would drastically impact our finances without first talking to us. I would soon learn that I was dead wrong.

As we moved into 2023, I began having an overwhelming feeling that something was wrong. I expressed this to Cara on numerous occasions, saying it was similar to the feeling I had just before having back surgery on March 1, 2011, the surgery that changed the course of my life for the worse. Cara listened to me, but she just didn't understand how powerful and upsetting this omen-like feeling could be. And, at the time, I could tell that Cara was slipping back into a depressed state, like she had done after the death of her mother. So, instead of focusing on my concerns, I tried to ignore them and help Cara with her depression.

Since her mother's death, Cara had been talking about how she missed her childhood, and on some of her darker days, she stated that she wanted to leave here and go be with her parents in heaven. I knew it was the depression, and it deeply concerned me, but I didn't know how to help her. Then, one Sunday morning, I noticed that Cara seemed to be more depressed than usual, so I decided to try something different.

"Cara, maybe you should think about calling Renee and telling her that you would like to go to church with her," I suggested.

Renee had previously invited Cara to attend church with her, but Cara hadn't accepted the offer.

"I've actually been thinking about it," she replied.

I nodded. "I really think that going back to church is what you need right now."

As we continued discussing the topic, I could see a small spark of hope in her, and she actually began feeling better as the day progressed.

Within a few days, Cara texted Renee and accepted her offer to attend church with her. Renee was happy to hear from Cara, and the two of them made plans to meet at church the following Sunday morning. I was so hopeful that attending church again would help Cara's mood improve.

It had only been a few weeks since Cara had started in church again, and I could see a big difference in her mood. She and Renee were going to church and then out for lunch almost every Sunday. Cara then learned that the church offered a Bible study for women on Tuesday mornings, and she was considering attending the classes. I thought it was a great idea and encouraged her to check it out, which she did. I was so grateful to see how happy all this was making her. It was nice to see her feeling so good about life again.

One Sunday after Cara returned from church, we talked about how well it was going and how much she enjoyed it. It was during this conversation that I mentioned the possibility of therapy to her.

"I would almost bet that a church that size probably offers counseling services," I said.

She said she wasn't sure, but that she would look into it to see if counseling was available.

On Tuesday, July 11, 2023, Cara was at her Bible study class when the doorbell rang. Our postal delivery man was at the door with certified mail that required a signature. After signing for it, I noticed that it was from Cara's sister Gwen. I found it suspicious that Gwen mailed the envelope from Edmond the previous day as an overnight delivery to Yukon when she knew that Cara would be in Bible study and that I would be home and have to sign for the package. I also noticed that Gwen mailed it on the anniversary of the death of my sister. But I'm sure that, as a good Christian, Gwen didn't mean anything by these two things.

I opened the envelope to see a check for forty-five thousand dollars. Now, at this point, most people would have been ecstatic about this amount of money. And I would have been ecstatic had I been told in advance about the money, so I could have made other plans regarding our stock investments. However, the envelope also contained a letter explaining the check, which came from closing out Dean's 401k and splitting the money between her three daughters. And because Gwen had inadvertently forgotten to include Dean's 401k in her trust, an account that she and Steve controlled, the money was not an inheritance and would need to be shown as income and taxes paid in full.

As I already stated, Cara and Gwen are very close. And Cara knew I had been working on a tax plan that would allow me to sell off a stock I bought at a rock-bottom price in 2020. Because we were retired and only showing our retirement incomes and interest, I would have been able to sell off over $100,000 in profits without paying one cent in capital gains tax. But now, because Gwen had neglected to speak to us about it, I had to hold off selling the stock for at least another year, possibly two.

I have since learned that self-appointed matriarchs don't need permission to destroy your financial plans. When I asked Cara about it, she said she didn't know anything about it, and she didn't know why Gwen did things the way she did or why she didn't reach out to us before making a decision that would greatly impact our finances.

The good news was that I thought I had finally found the cause of the overwhelming feelings I'd had since earlier in the year. Once again, this would prove to be incorrect.

It took me a couple of days to accept the changes that had been thrust upon me. After thinking about it, I came up with a new financial plan that I could make work. Unfortunately, the stressors of life had worsened the inguinal hernia on my right side, and it looked like I would require surgery to repair the hernia. Thankfully, my primary care physician got me right in and referred me to a surgeon in the same building.

When Cara and I met with the surgeon, he explained that I actually had two inguinal hernias, but the one on my left side was still fairly minor. And, thanks to previous CT scans of my chest, he was able to show me the difference between the two hernias. He did say that the hernia on the right side was worse and that although surgery was recommended, it was not required at the moment. He further explained that surgery may actually never be needed and that the odds of the hernia rupturing were minimal. Therefore, at least for the time being, it was safe to postpone surgery indefinitely, which I decided to do. At that time, I had eight surgeries under my belt, and I really didn't want to add one more to the list.

Cara and I had a few weeks that seemed to be fairly quiet but, once again, I now realize that it was just the calm before the storm. By August 2023, Cara had learned that the church did offer counseling services, so she scheduled her first session. It would be a couple of weeks before she met with the counselor, but after returning home from the session, she was excited about how well it had gone and couldn't wait until her next session the following week. I was so happy that everything was working out for her and that she was doing so well managing the depression.

The following week seemed very routine until Cara returned from her second counseling session. I wasn't sure what was wrong, but I could definitely tell something was off-kilter. Cara had seemed so happy when she left for her session that morning, but she now seemed upset. I asked her about it, and she reassured me that she was okay, but it was obvious she wasn't. I tried to engage in conversation, but she just didn't seem interested in talking to me. I decided to leave her alone for a while and went into the office and got on the computer.

After waiting a few hours, I came back into the living room, where Cara was sitting on the couch looking depressed.

"Cara, what's wrong?" I asked.

"I don't know."

"Is it me?"

"I don't know," she repeated.

I didn't understand what was going on, but if I was causing her to feel this way, I needed to know. Sadly, to this day, I'm not sure why I stated it to her the way I did.

"Cara, if it's me that's making you unhappy," I started cautiously, "please let me know and we'll come up with an exit strategy." I truly believed that we were one of the few couples in the world that would never give up on our relationship. After all, we had assured each other of that for the past fifteen and a half years, telling each other numerous times that we would never give up on us and that we would be together until one of us died. But then her words destroyed my world.

"Yes, that's it," she said. "I want a divorce."

"No, this can't be happening," I vaguely remember saying.

I don't remember much of what happened after that, but I do remember having a panic attack that was so bad I had to take medication to get it under control. I do know that I was in denial and didn't understand what was happening. The love of my life, my soulmate, the person I trusted more than anyone else on this planet, the person who assured me she would never give up on us, just said the words that caused me to feel like my soul was burning. And I didn't understand why this was happening. To this day, I'm left with so many unanswered questions.

At the beginning of my story, I quoted Oscar Wilde and said I understood the first part of his quote about not getting what we want. But now, I sincerely understood the *second* part his quote, about getting what we want. Unfortunately, I also learned that the pain affiliated with getting what we want can be much more devastating than the pain of not getting what we want.

As a reminder, here's Oscar Wilde's quote in its entirety.

"There are only two tragedies in life: one is not getting what one wants, and the other is getting it."

A Never-Ending Nightmare

If you have ever, even for a moment, felt like your life had become intertwined with a Stephen King horror novel, then you may understand what I experienced over the next several months. And for those of you fortunate enough to have never experienced that feeling, I hope you never do.

In the first few weeks after learning that Cara wanted a divorce, I felt numb and had trouble functioning on most days. Now, I was the one who was suffering from depression, while she was getting stronger by the day. It was as if she had forced her negative energy into me and taken my "the glass is always half full" spirit away. Yes, I know how insane that sounds, but it's what I was feeling at the time. The hardest part to deal with was the fact that I was trying to help her overcome her depression when the world flipped upside down on me.

I had experienced the phrase "no good deed goes unpunished" multiple times during my lifetime, but never anything at this level, and especially not by the person who had assured me she was never going anywhere. She, more than any other person, had seen the emotional scars that I've lived with for so many years, and now, she was doing more damage to me than I have ever imagined possible. I still struggle with how this sweet Christian lady, who could never hurt anyone, changed in an instant. But, as I've since learned, that is exactly what happened right before my eyes.

After I pushed through the numbness and darkness of the first few days, Cara and I sat down together and attempted to work out all the details. To help hold down the additional expenses, we wanted to try and work through the divorce without hiring two attorneys. I already knew that not only would this turn out to be the most devastating emotional loss I had ever experienced, but because I had relented and combined our finances, it would also be the largest financial loss I had ever experienced. Therefore, using one attorney seemed like the best move for both of us.

Some of the things I was experiencing sounded crazy, even to me. I told Cara one day that it felt like my soulmate, lover, and best friend had gone to church for a therapy session one morning and then, like a scene out of a sci-fi movie, walked through a portal into another dimension and one of Satan's demons came back in her place. I truly didn't know this person anymore, and her behavior really was bizarre at times.

"Cara, you once told me that your grandmother divorced your grandfather when she was about our age. Is there some weird connection between you and your grandmother that I'm missing?" I asked her.

"No, but thanks for bringing it up," she snapped back at me.

"I'm not trying to upset you. I'm just trying to understand what the hell is happening to us," I tried to explain. "I know you don't get it, but because of everything we've been through together, I believed you when you told me that we would be together until one of us died. And now, you're leaving me at the worst possible time in my life. I need you now more than ever, and the Cara I've known for the past twenty years wouldn't do this to me."

"I'm sorry," she said.

No matter how many of these conversations we would have, she would always just tell me that she was sorry, and that would be the end of it.

Having previously gone through two divorces, I understood that a divorce could bring out the worst in people, but this was different. I had never witnessed a transformation like this before in my life. And because of all the bizarre changes I soon noticed, I began second-guessing the entire past twenty years of our lives together.

As much as I hate to admit it, some days I truly had difficulty differentiating between reality and some sci-fi horror movie where I was playing the starring role. I kept telling myself that I was still in shock and that my mind was just having difficulty processing the changes. But shock couldn't explain all of it away.

One of the first changes I noticed was Cara's snoring. For as long as I have known her, Cara has had severe problems with snoring. At times, it was so bad that it would wake us both from a deep sleep and often scare her. She had been tested and treated with a BiPAP machine, which did help, but she eventually got tired of dealing with the mask and stopped using it. She had also been seen by an otolaryngologist, who prescribed nose drops, which didn't help at all. Fortunately, we found nose strips that did help, and Cara virtually stopped snoring. She used the strips nightly for the next few years, which allowed both of us to finally get some uninterrupted sleep.

Cara and I continued to live like we had done before she decided to get divorced, including sharing a bed. Because our routine hadn't changed, one morning as I was getting out of bed, I noticed that she wasn't wearing a nose strip. And yet, she hadn't been snoring. My first thought was that it must have fallen off during the night, so I didn't question it. However, I began noticing that she wasn't wearing the strips at all, and yet she wasn't snoring. I didn't understand how this was possible, but I waited a little longer to watch and see if I was missing something.

After a week or so with no snoring, I asked her why she wasn't wearing the nose strips, and she simply stated that she no longer needed them. When I pushed the issue, she finally said that she had begun using the nose drops and that they were working. However, I knew that the nose drops had never worked, and I also knew she wasn't using them.

Although this wasn't proof of anything, other than the fact that she was lying to me and that she no longer snored while sleeping, it was just one more inexplicable change I had noticed about her during our final months together.

The next change I noticed had to do with her recurring nightmares. Again, for as long as I've known Cara, she has always suffered from nightmares that would cause her to cry out for help, which always woke me up. I learned to gently wake her and reassure her that it was just a bad dream. Every time, it was the same type of dream. She would tell me that someone was trying to get her, chasing her or holding her down. But a few months after she started attending The Bridge Church, which is an Assemblies of God church, Cara sat up in bed one night (sitting up during a nightmare was a first for her) and began speaking gibberish. In a very loud, almost yelling, demanding voice, she repeated an unintelligible phrase over and over again until I woke her up.

Having attended an Assembly of God church for a while as a kid, I was vaguely familiar with members speaking in tongues, which is what I first thought she was doing. When I asked her if she had heard anyone speak in tongues at the church, she said she had witnessed a few members speaking in tongues over the past few months. I then asked her if she remembered what the dream was about and what she was saying. She explained that she was telling someone to stop hurting someone else, but she didn't know who those people were. When I told her that it sounded like she was repeating a phrase very loudly, she seemed sincerely surprised and couldn't explain it. By this time, I was becoming very upset with the church and its members, so I spoke up.

"Cara, what the hell is going on at that church?" I asked her.

"Nothing's going on," she replied. "It was just a nightmare."

"No, that wasn't just a nightmare," I fired back. "I've been waking you up from nightmares for almost two decades and you've never done anything like this before."

I further explained that I was growing very concerned about her safety, but she didn't seem to care about anything I had to say. She lay back down and went to sleep.

Out of curiosity, I searched online for videos of people speaking in tongues. After listening to various soundtracks, I'm still unsure of what Cara uttered that night, but it definitely didn't sound like she was simply speaking in tongues. She repeatedly said something that sounded like a phrase. And for the first time, I was the one who felt afraid when waking her from a nightmare.

As we were attempting to work through the details of the divorce, Cara reminded me that if I didn't have the bilateral inguinal hernia surgery before she left, I would be on my own once she moved out. I reminded her that I had already gone through eight surgeries, five of which were during our time together, and that I really didn't want to go through another one. However, after thinking about the consequences of trying to recover alone from a major surgery, I reluctantly agreed to schedule the surgery before she moved out.

"We have tickets to see Joe Bonamassa on November 5," I said. "Are you okay with me scheduling the surgery after that date?"

"Yes, that's fine," she replied.

I scheduled the surgery for Friday, November 10, 2023, and then I tried to forget about it. I had front-row tickets to see Bonamassa and, because that was the only positive thing in my life at that time, I tried to think only about the concert and block out everything negative. I wish it had been that easy.

I began noticing that Cara was spending a lot of time communicating with someone on her phone. If I asked too many questions, she would tell me that she had a headache, or she wasn't feeling well and wanted to go lie down, which had become a frequent occurrence. However, when I would go into the bedroom and see she was texting with someone, she would lie and say she was just looking at photos on Pinterest.

"Cara, please stop lying to me," I begged. "You and I both know that when you're on Pinterest, you don't type with both thumbs. If you're seeing someone, please don't lie about it."

"I'm not seeing anyone," she defended herself. "I sometimes text with Gwen."

"Okay, then show me the texts."

"I'm actually on Instagram."

"That's fine. Show me the DMs."

"I delete them as soon as we're done."

"Just how fucking stupid do you think I am, Cara? You and I both know that you're lying."

I could feel myself becoming so angry, I knew it wasn't going to end well and decided to walk away. But I did speak my mind one last time before exiting the room.

"I spent over fifteen years telling everyone that you were the best Christian I'd ever known. But now, I realize you're just another lying hypocrite."

The saddest part is that she didn't seem to care that she was lying to me with every breath. I don't think I'll ever understand how she lied so easily.

Over the next several weeks, Cara was in constant communication with someone, but I didn't know who. More than once, I became frustrated and told her I'd had enough of it, but she threatened me with leaving before my surgery. I knew if I pushed too hard, I'd be recovering from the surgery alone, so I had to bite my tongue on numerous occasions.

At other times, she would tell me she was going to read her Bible or one of her Christian books and go into the bedroom to be alone. She would sit on the bed, leaning against the headboard with her legs bent up, holding the book on her lap. I eventually realized she had her phone in between the pages of the book, and she wasn't actually reading. I think it angered me so much because she used religion to hide what she was doing.

I tried to accept that the person in our home wasn't the person I had known for nearly two decades, and I just stayed out of our bedroom until it was time to go to bed. It eventually became easier to let it go instead of putting her in a position where she felt like she needed to lie to me. And I guess I did as well as any hurting human could have done—until the night of the Bonamassa concert.

We arrived early and located our seats, which were unbelievably close to the stage. Joe was my second favorite guitarist on the planet before Eddie Van Halen died. After Eddie's death, Joe moved up into the number one position. And although I had already seen him perform live, this time I would get to see him from the front row.

To avoid any potential issues, I explained to Cara how important this night was for me and asked her to please not be texting with anyone. She agreed, and I was hopeful that she would keep her word. Sadly, I guess I was just a fool for believing that anyone willing to constantly lie would actually be honest even for just one night.

The show was amazing, and Cara kept her phone away during the entire concert, which allowed me to truly enjoy Bonamassa and the band. However, when the concert was over and we were leaving, I stopped by the restroom. Cara found a table with a chair, sat down and said she would be waiting for me. I walked down toward the restroom, but when I saw how long the line was, I decided to wait until we got home. I turned around and walked back to where Cara was waiting for me. Maybe I should have expected her to be on her phone, but once again, I was a fool for believing her.

As I walked up to the table, I saw that she was typing very quickly with both thumbs, so I just stood there and stared at her. It took her a few seconds before she realized that I was standing in front of her. For the first time, I saw fear in her eyes as the blood drained from her face.

She immediately stopped, and using one finger, she closed the app. I just continued staring at her and didn't say a word.

"That was fast," she commented.

"The line was too long. I can wait until we get home."

She put her phone away, and we walked out of the building. When we got in the car, I asked her, "Who were you communicating with, Cara?"

"I wasn't communicating with anyone. I was just checking to see if Nate had posted anything new to his Instagram."

Nate is her niece's husband. I knew Cara was lying. I think she said Nate's name instead of her niece Lauren just in case I happened to see a man's photo.

"You couldn't even let me have one last night, could you?" I asked.

"I wasn't doing anything wrong," Cara exclaimed.

"When you and I made the mistake of having an affair while I was married to Lorrie, we both swore that we would never hurt another human being again," I reminded her. "Just for the record, I kept my word to you."

We sat quietly for a long while as we drove home before finally speaking again.

"I know I must be the biggest fool in the world, but I truly believed that the only mistake you have ever made was having an affair with me," I started. "And sadly, I also believed that you would never do anything like this again in your life. But I was wrong. I know that I deserve everything that's happening to me, but I never thought you would be the one to hurt me."

She didn't reply to anything I said, so I stopped talking for the rest of the drive home. It was one of the most painful nights of my life and I felt like I wanted to break down and cry, but I didn't.

I guess I let the depression get the best of me after that incident, because all week I prayed to the universe that I wouldn't make it off the surgery table alive on Friday. This was going to be my ninth surgery, I was losing the one person I thought would never betray me, and I had reached my breaking point. I was ready to get the hell off this damn rock. But I guess the universe wasn't willing to let me go home, and I did wake up after the surgery. Now, I would have to suffer through another long, painful recovery. For the next several weeks, I kept asking myself and the universe when the suffering would finally end. But I never did receive an answer.

In the first three days after the surgery, Cara got up each morning and helped me get situated in the recliner with my coffee. However, on the fourth day, as I was getting out of bed, I noticed that Cara wasn't getting up.

"Let me know if you need any help," she said.

"Are you kidding me?" I snarked at her. "Yes, I need your help, Cara."

I know how hard it is for Cara to get up early in the morning, but I was becoming very irritated, which is the worst thing you can do when you're in a lot of pain.

"Okay, I'm getting up," she groaned.

"I know this is hard on you, but I shouldn't have to ask you for help on day four after a major surgery."

It was obvious I was pissed, but I'm not sure she really cared.

"I said I'm getting up," she repeated as she got out of bed and walked around to my side.

After making it to the living room, Cara helped me get situated before asking if I needed anything else. I said I was good for now, and she returned to bed. At that moment, I knew I would need to start trying to do more on my own.

It was later that evening, and I had moved over to the softer loveseat. Cara was reclining on the larger couch, and we were watching television when her phone rang.

"It's Renee," she said after answering it.

The two of them began talking, and within a few minutes, Cara was laughing like a little school-girl. This surprised me because, until recently, Cara would always comment about how some women never seemed to grow up and acted like they were still in high school. I couldn't believe what I was hearing. Again, this was a change I never saw coming. Who the hell was this person who used to be my soulmate?

After a few more minutes of the giggling, I finally said something to her.

"Cara, will you please call her back later, so I can relax tonight?" I asked.

She glared at me and then I heard her say, "Renee, I'm going to have to call you later. Kenny doesn't want me talking to you right now."

I couldn't believe what I had just witnessed. I was four days out of surgery, I needed some peace and quiet to recover, and she just played the victim while making me out to be the villain.

"Did you have to say it like that?" I asked.

"Like what?"

"Please don't play dumb with me. You know what the hell you just did."

"You wanted me off the phone and I got off the phone. What's the problem?" she retorted.

"Cara, do you not have enough decency left in you to act like you at least used to care about me? All you had to do was tell her that I'm not feeling well and that I would like some time to recover."

"I'm off the phone, so you got what you wanted," she snarled.

I knew it wasn't going to get any better, so I just let it go. And, once again, I wished I had been alone so I could cry and get it out of my system. But I wasn't alone, and I didn't cry.

I'm not sure if my brain finally connected the dots or if the universe whispered in my ear, but about an hour after Cara got off the phone with Renee, I started thinking about what Lorrie had said many years earlier. I remembered what Lorrie had told me about Cara being gay back before we got married. I had asked Cara about it, and she'd assured me it wasn't true, so I had let it go. But now, I was second-guessing everything. I was afraid to say anything, so I kept watching the show and thought of how I wanted to approach the topic.

After the show was over, I decided to try and talk to Cara about it.

I turned to her. "Cara, before we got married," I calmly started, "I asked you if you were gay, and you assured me that you are not. I told you that it was Lorrie who told me. But what I didn't tell you is that she actually hired a private investigator to do a background check on you, and that's how she learned about you living in a one-bedroom apartment with another woman for about ten years."

Before I could get out another word, Cara erupted.

"That fucking whore!" she screamed at the top of her lungs.

I had never heard Cara use that kind of language or yell that loudly. I realized I had struck a nerve, and I knew better than to say another word. The room went silent. We both just stared at the television without speaking. Then, after a while, we got up and went to bed.

As I lay in bed, my mind was jumping between Cara divorcing me because I'm not a Christian, to her having an affair with a man, and then to the possibility that she's gay. Then I would start the cycle all over again. It was truly the nightmare from hell, and I couldn't wake myself up.

Cara was upset with me because I questioned her sexuality, and I was so confused about everything happening in my life. I guess if I learned anything from this experience, it's to never undergo major surgery while going through a divorce. If I had known how it would all play out, I would have postponed the surgery until after the divorce was finalized and then found another way to deal with the recovery.

As I slowly began feeling better, we returned to the process of working through the divorce. Because I had decided to stay in our home, I asked Cara to put together a list of all the items she would be taking with her. Her list turned out to be rather short. At first I was a little surprised, until I reminded myself that she would be leaving with close to half a million dollars in cash, which would be more than enough money to purchase all new furniture for her apartment.

In December, we reached out to an attorney to help us complete the paperwork. However, Cara and I didn't realize it would take so long to finalize the process.

We called the attorney's office every couple of weeks for an update, but we were always given a different reason why it was taking so long. We were first told that the attorney was ill, then her son had to have an unscheduled surgery, then she was undergoing physical therapy for an injury, and finally, she was gone on vacation. At one point, it dawned on me that the divorce wouldn't be finalized until sometime in March, and I told that to Cara.

"Why do you think it will be March?" she asked.

"Because that's when big events seem to happen in my life," I replied.

"Well, let's hope it doesn't take that long," she said, very matter-of-factly.

In the meantime, hoping that the divorce wouldn't take until March, Cara began boxing up the items on her list and storing them in our bedroom. I knew she was moving out, but having to walk by the packed boxes every day was just another reminder of how I had screwed up my life by not listening to that little voice.

During the six-month period between September 2023 and March 2024, which was the time from when Cara told me that she wanted a divorce to the time that she moved out, I had more than a couple of dark days when I felt extremely unstable. On those occasions, when I couldn't stop my mind from going to a dark place, I asked Cara if she would please go spend a few days with her sister Gwen. I even told her that I was more unstable than I had ever felt in my life, and I thought it would be best for both of us if she would please let me have some downtime. However, regardless of how I expressed my mental status to her, Cara would always tell me that she wasn't leaving until she had the money in her bank account, and I would always tell her that I wasn't dividing the money until the divorce had been finalized.

Cara would also tell me that she didn't want to be a burden on Gwen. But no matter how many excuses she used, I knew she would be moving in with Gwen when she left here, at least for a while.

"Cara, you haven't even rented an apartment, which tells me that you are moving in with Gwen," I pointed out.

"I'm still waiting for the apartment manager to call me with a move-in date," she said.

"You know there's no reason to continue lying about it. We both know you're going straight to Gwen's when you leave here."

I never understood why she continued to deny it until a couple of weeks before she moved out. Then, she finally admitted that she was going to stay with Gwen for a while. I don't understand why she lied about something so insignificant. I didn't give a damn where she would be living after she moved out.

I now understand that lying and fighting become the norm when you're going through a divorce. Even for a couple who once believed they were soulmates. This is just one more reason why couples should not live together during that time. I understand that many couples can't afford to live apart, but it was never about the money for us. We had enough money to afford two places and we both had access to all of it. There was just no excuse for the decisions we made during our final six months together.

When I reflect on that time, I still don't understand why we stayed in the same house, slept in the same bed and even continued being intimate. That is, when we weren't arguing with each other. I've often asked myself if it was because I was so in love with her that I just wanted to be near her, while she was simply keeping an eye on the money. I still don't know for sure. I am, however, grateful that when I was feeling so unstable, I didn't cross the line and do something I couldn't take back. Who knows, maybe I have finally begun listening to that little voice that tries to protect us from ourselves.

It's painfully obvious to me that I've been my own worst enemy in this lifetime, and it always points directly back to not listening to that little voice. If some scientists are correct about multiverses, I really hope that in one of them, I started listening to that little voice when I was young.

As I had predicted, the divorce was finalized on March 6, 2024, which meant that we were married for sixteen years, beginning and ending in the month of March. (If that sounds familiar, it's because I worked for the University of Oklahoma for sixteen years, beginning and ending in the month of March.)

After the divorce had been finalized, I asked Cara when she planned on moving out, and she said it would be on Saturday, March 23. I thought the date sounded familiar, but I couldn't remember why. Then, after a few days, it dawned on me that this was the same date my divorce from Lorrie was finalized in 2007. One more "coincidence" to keep my mind reeling, but not the strangest thing that would happen over the next couple of weeks.

With only a short while left together, I asked Cara about a few of the items on her list.

"Do you have some space in one of your boxes to pack the two crosses?"

"I'm not taking them with me," she replied.

"What do you mean, you're not taking them?" I asked, baffled.

"I don't want them. If you don't want them, you can get rid of them."

"Cara, the crosses are on the wall for you, and you added them to the list of items you're taking," I tried to explain.

"I just don't want them," she reiterated.

I could understand her changing her mind about the cross on the dining room wall. We picked it up at a charity auction, and it didn't have special meaning to her. But, the beautiful cross on our living room wall was a gift from family friends she had known since childhood. She and her two sisters all received identical crosses when their mother died. It was a special gift, and leaving it behind didn't make sense to me. I still remember how surprised and excited Cara was when the package arrived at our home shortly after the death of her mother. She wanted the cross mounted in the living room immediately.

I agreed to keep them and told Cara to just leave them where they were if she didn't want them. I am no longer a Christian, but to me, the cross still holds a powerful, beautiful meaning. When I see a cross, I am immediately reminded of the story of one man who was willing to give up his life to save others. Whether it actually happened is irrelevant to me; it's about the story it represents. And that's why both crosses are still hung up in my home.

Cara also left behind a beautifully framed photo of the Lord's Prayer, which is still hanging on the wall leading into the master bedroom. When I asked her why she was leaving all the religious items behind, she simply said she didn't want them anymore. As much as I didn't want to climb aboard Ozzy's Crazy Train, that little voice was telling me that something was seriously wrong in this universe. And a few days later, I would continue to see a pattern that still mystifies me to this day.

When the divorce had been finalized, we began completing the tasks on Cara's list, which included moving money into her new accounts and adding her new credit card information to the online accounts that she would need to begin paying each month. Because I was the one who always handled our finances, I agreed to help her with these tasks and teach her how it was done.

As we were setting up Cara's first online payment, I asked her for her credit card number, but she didn't reply.

"I'm ready for the number." I repeated.

"You're going to love this," she smirked.

I didn't understand what she was referencing, so I ignored her and waited for her to give me the number.

"I'm ready," I said, I looked at her and then back at the computer screen.

As she began reading the number, I understood what she meant.

I stopped entering the number. "You're not serious?" I asked.

"Yes, that's the number."

"Your new card number has 666 in it, and you're keeping the card?"

"It doesn't bother me," she said. "You're the one that it bothers."

"It's because of what it represents, Cara," I pointed out. "It doesn't matter if it's true, everyone knows that it represents the number of the beast. You're really going to keep the card?" I asked her again.

"Yes," she firmly replied.

I looked at the card to see if she was just messing with me, but she wasn't. Three sixes in a row, not four, just three. At that moment, my mind began racing with unimaginable thoughts as to why Cara wasn't taking any of the Christian-based items from our home. Bewildered, I handed the card back to her and continued entering the number.

Once we had completed setting up all her online accounts, I turned to look at her. "The Cara I married would never have kept this card. She would have returned it and requested a new one. I honestly don't know who the hell you are."

She didn't reply, and we never talked about it again.

Yellow Cake, Chocolate Icing

We had reached our final night together, and I decided to stay up for a while when Cara went to bed.

"What time should I wake you up in the morning?" I asked her.

"Will you get me up at six?"

"Yes."

"Good night," she said as she got up and put on her house shoes.

"Good night, Cara. I won't be much longer."

"Okay, I'll see you in a little bit." She turned and walked to our bedroom.

I knew it would be the last night we would ever spend together, but I couldn't make myself go to bed. I just needed to sit quietly and process all of it for a while.

When I finally made myself go to bed, I was restless the entire night. I only slept for a few hours before I was back up, drinking coffee in the recliner in the dimly lit living room.

I was closely watching the clock to ensure I woke her up on time, when I was startled by Cara entering the room.

"I'm sorry," she said. "I didn't mean to scare you."

"It's okay. My mind is some other place right now."

"Will you come back to bed?" she asked me.

By the look on my face, she could tell I didn't understand what she was asking of me.

"I want to be with you," she continued.

"You mean, intimate?" I asked.

"Yes."

"You know I will, Cara."

I was stunned by her request, but grateful at the same time. And there was no way that I was going to turn down her offer. I still loved her so much, and I didn't want her to leave. In fact, I would have done almost anything to make it work with her. But I guess it just wasn't meant to be, at least not in this universe.

After we made love, she laid her head on my shoulder and quietly cried for the longest time. I didn't understand then, and I don't understand now, but I don't think I'll ever forget how it felt when her tears rolled off her face onto my chest.

Within a few hours, Cara's nephews arrived with a pickup truck to help move her boxes to Gwen's house. After the boxes were loaded and her nephews left, Cara and I talked for a while before saying our final goodbyes.

After Cara drove away and I was alone in the house, I thought this would finally be the time I would break down and cry it all out of my system, but I didn't. Instead, I made a double-layered yellow cake with chocolate icing, grabbed a fork and began eating it.

Not once did I cut a piece and eat it like a normal person. Instead, over the next few days, I would pick up a fork and eat as much cake as I wanted before putting it away again. I would do this until the cake was gone. Admittedly, it only took me a few days to finish it off, but I enjoyed every bite!

Epilogue

Several months ago, I began journaling as a form of therapy, which has significantly helped calm my mind and allowed me to focus on more positive aspects of my life. I couldn't always see it, but I now understand just how emotionally damaged and lost I had become after Cara moved out. And, because I'm honestly baring my soul, I have to admit that on a couple of occasions, during my darkest hours, I came very close to checking out permanently and getting the hell out of here.

It's still not easy to admit it, but losing my soulmate took something from me that I'll never get back. Not to mention the trust issues I'll be dealing with for the rest of my life. After all, I already had trust issues that made it difficult to trust almost anyone. When I did finally allow myself to fully trust Cara, she took advantage of that trust and betrayed me on a level I would never have believed was possible. I only wish I knew her true motives for her betrayal.

Most surprisingly, I've learned that after months of journaling, I still don't have the answers I thought I'd find. I guess I believed that by reliving, processing and documenting my life with Cara, I'd somehow magically find the answers to all my questions, especially to all the strange behavior I witnessed during our final six months of marriage. But it didn't happen. That's not to say I didn't learn anything from this experience, because I did.

I learned the importance of listening to that little voice when it speaks to me. I can only imagine how different my life might be today if I had learned to listen to that voice long before meeting Cara.

I learned just how tough karma can be when it comes back around. That old saying, "Karma is a bitch," is a massive understatement. My karma has been tougher than I could have ever imagined. That's not to say I don't deserve everything that has happened to me. I do, and I accept my fate.

I learned the most painful betrayals come from the ones we trust the most. I've never trusted anyone like I trusted Cara. And I've never been betrayed by anyone like I was betrayed by Cara.

Just as importantly, I learned that when something seems too good to be true, it probably is. I believed Cara was the epitome of goodness. She possessed an innocence about her I'd never seen before. Unfortunately, I now know that Cara's portrayal of the girl next door was all part of a bigger plan that I couldn't see at the time. And sadly, she proved she didn't care who she hurt to get the life she wanted.

Lastly, I learned that inviting darkness into your life doesn't always involve a pentagram and an invitation from the Prince of Darkness himself. Sometimes—as in my situation—it begins with good intentions and innocent missteps that lead to bad decisions. I truly believed that if darkness entered my life, it would be easy to see. But again, I was wrong. I had no idea it could appear from nowhere and be disguised as a shy, quiet Christian girl from next door.

I previously mentioned that I'm a spiritual agnostic who no longer practices religion. I do, however, believe the words written by Paul the Apostle in 2 Corinthians 11:14-15. The New International Version translation is:

"And no wonder, for Satan himself masquerades as an angel of light. It is not surprising, then, if his servants also masquerade as servants of righteousness."

Based on Paul's words, I can't think of a better way to hide in plain sight than to live your life as a Christian.

At some point during my journey of discovery, I couldn't help but wonder how many others have experienced situations similar to mine. Considering it's been almost 2,000 years since Paul wrote 2 Corinthians, darkness masquerading as righteousness is obviously not anything new. I then began thinking that if I shared my story with others, maybe it could prevent someone from making the same mistakes I made. And, more importantly, maybe it could prevent someone from experiencing the betrayal and loss I experienced.

To wrap up, I believe I can best sum up my experience with Cara by using three Joe Bonamassa songs. The first is "Self-Inflicted Wounds." As the title implies, I've learned I have often been my own worst enemy. The second song is "Sloe Gin," which I think best describes the current status of my life. I'm still suffering and trying to learn how to grow from the pain.

Finally, the third song is "Redemption." Although I've made a mess of my life, I do still have hope that one day I will find redemption.

www.ingramcontent.com/pod-product-compliance
Lightning Source LLC
LaVergne TN
LVHW091048150826
845673LV00002B/498

* 9 7 9 8 2 3 0 5 1 2 4 6 2 *